Successful
Web Marketing for the
TOURISM and
LEISURE SECTORS

Successful
Web Marketing for the
TOURISM and
LEISURE SECTORS

SUSAN BRIGGS

**KOGAN
PAGE**

To Nina, born into a world full of technology, which still needs magic and dreams. May they all come true.

First published in 2001 by Kogan Page Limited

Kogan Page Limited
120 Pentonville Road
London N1 9JN

British Library Cataloguing in Publication Data

A CIP record for this book is available from the British Library.

ISBN 0 7494 3586 0

Typeset by JS Typesetting, Wellingborough, Northants
Printed and bound in Great Britain by Biddles Ltd, Guildford and King's Lynn
www.biddles.co.uk

CONTENTS

ACKNOWLEDGEMENTS

Thanks are especially due to Mary and Malcolm for their loving support, together with Elias for his technical expertise and ability to 'mend things'.

Thanks are also due to CACI Ltd for their information on E-Types and to MarketVoice, Paul Chibeba and Penny Williams at the South East England Tourist Board for permission to use their research, commissioned jointly with the Southern Tourist Board, about the role of the Internet in destination marketing.

INTRODUCTION

The Internet has already become an essential promotional tool for the tourism and leisure industry. Travel is one of the fastest-growing and most commercially successful sectors of e-commerce. Research companies predict that by 2005 the online leisure travel market will grow from the current £592 million to more than £3.7 billion. This vast figure does not take account of business travel or domestic leisure and tourism activity such as visits to the theatre, sporting events and so on which will also be booked online.

Over the past five years, there has been exponential growth in the number of tourism and leisure-related Web sites, ranging from portals developed by tourist boards and consortia to simple stand-alone sites by independent hoteliers and attractions. And yet Internet marketing is still in its infancy.

Many Web sites were originally developed as a 'me-too/must-have' reaction, rather than as part of a considered, integrated marketing strategy. Second-generation Web sites are more likely to take advantage of some of the benefits of marketing on the Internet. But more often than not, it is a case of expensive trial and error.

It is easy to find information about how to use the net as a surfer and how to develop Web sites from a technical perspective. It can be more difficult to find tangible advice on the impact of the Internet, how it is changing the marketing world and how you can benefit from it.

This book aims to help leisure and tourism organizations to develop better Web sites and make them part of their overall marketing campaign. It considers the changing profile of Internet users, as well as some of the most important trends and changes likely to affect tourism and leisure companies. It then looks at the use of the Internet as a promotional tool and how it can be integrated into your marketing strategy, as well as offering concrete advice on how to promote your site and use the Internet for direct marketing.

The final section shows some practical examples of good Web sites and details of useful sites for research and marketing purposes. Please note that due to the fast-developing nature of the internet, some of the sites given as examples may have changed. Details of particular Web sites do not represent a recommendation.

In order to avoid confusion between visitors in the Internet and tourism senses, this book refers throughout to Internet 'users' and tourism 'visitors'.

UNTANGLING THE WEB

This chapter aims to help you understand how the Internet works and why it is such a powerful marketing medium. It outlines some of the technical developments that are contributing to the growing power of the Internet and some of the issues likely to affect its future evolution.

There are many books dealing with the technical aspects of how the Internet works and how to design and develop Web sites. This explanation does not attempt to emulate those, but seeks to equip readers with sufficient information to help them to understand and use the power of the Internet to market to their customers. At the back of this book there is a glossary to help you understand some of the jargon associated with the Internet.

HOW THE INTERNET WORKS

The easiest way to imagine how the Internet works is to think of it as a massive collection of millions of computers linked together. Most people currently access the Internet through their computer using a phone line and modem which connects them to their Internet Service Provider (usually abbreviated to ISP).

ISPs then connect to each other to transfer information. Some of the largest ISPs are the 'backbone providers' for much larger networks, covering regions or even countries. They use fibre optic lines, with satellite links and cables under the sea so that all computers on the Internet are effectively connected to each other.

The fastest-growing part of the Internet (and the one which is likely to be of most interest to the tourism industry) is the World Wide Web (WWW or the Web). The Web is effectively a collection of easy-to-use Web sites (which are made up of Web pages), uploaded to the Internet and accessible 24 hours a day. Anyone browsing or 'surfing' the Internet can view these files and decide to access other pages by using their computer mouse to 'click' on relevant links.

Surfers typically use one of two 'browser' programs to view Web pages: either Microsoft's Internet Explorer or Netscape's Navigator. Think of these as the windows through which Web sites can be seen. Different versions of these browser programs

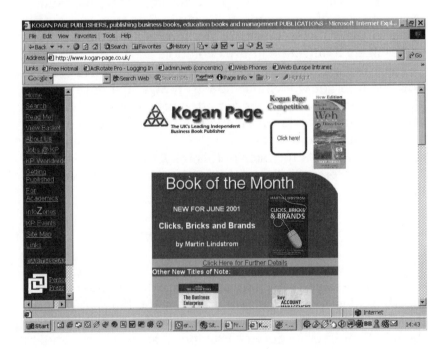

Figure 1.1   Web sites are available 24 hours a day and make use of internal and external *links* to provide extensive information and sales opportunities

are now also being developed so the Internet can be accessed through other devices such as mobile phones and personal digital assistants (PDAs), like the Palm Pilot or the Psion.

Web sites make use of 'links', either internally to other sections of the same Web site, or externally to other sites. It is these links which make the Web such an interactive medium. Unlike traditional print media where the reader has all the pages available and then decides which to read, the Internet does not present pages automatically to the viewer. Instead, it offers non-sequential access, meaning that users have to actually request pages by clicking on underlined link words or icons, rather than turning the page as they would with a book. Users browse through different sites and pages and switch from one to another. This means that they effectively demand the pages they wish to see, so they can be more selective.

The Internet can be used to search for information about almost anything in the world, make online purchases (frequently referred to as e-commerce), send e-mails, enter 'chatrooms' where users type messages to each other in real time, place a bet or play games ranging from chess to space invaders with friends or total strangers, and participate in newsgroups and other online communities.

There are three main ways in which people can find a Web site:

▓ They type the Web site address of a site they already know about, into the '**address**' line of their browser. The Web site address is called the '**domain name**' or the URL (Universal Resource Locator). Each Web site's address is as unique as someone's home address, so no two Web sites can share the same address.

▓ They use a 'search engine' or directory such as www.yahoo. co.uk or www.google.com to look up relevant sites. There is more information about search engines and how they work in chapter 8.

▓ They follow the links from another Web site.

The '**home page**' is usually the first or main page which a visitor to a Web site sees. A key element of the home page is the 'menu', similar to the index in a book, listing the links which can be followed to the rest of the site.

Some Web sites act as signposts or gateways to other relevant and related sites. These are known as '**portals**'. ISPs such as Freeserve generally have portal sites, but you can also find industry- or interest-specific sites which aim to be portals. There are, for example, the ones operated by national tourist boards like the British Tourist Authority, who have a site for visitors to Britain called www.visitbritain.com and another portal for tourism professionals called www.tourismtrade.org.uk. These specialist or industry-specific sites are sometimes called '**vortals**', short for vertical portals.

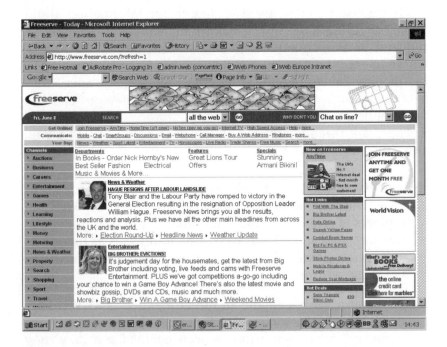

Figure 1.2 Most Internet Service Providers have *portal* sites like this one from Freeserve

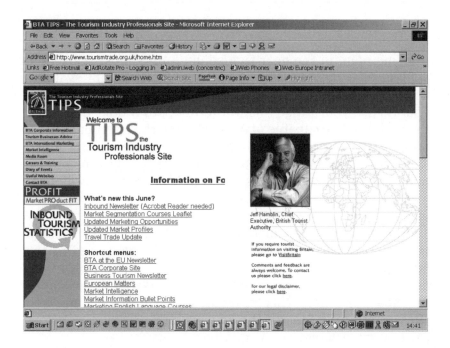

Figure 1.3 Industry-specific sites like this one are sometimes called *vortals*, short for 'vertical portals'

OVERVIEW OF TECHNICAL DEVELOPMENTS

The Internet is still evolving, so any detailed description of technical developments is likely to be at least partially out of date in the time it takes between writing and publishing this book. The following section deals with some of the most important developments currently taking place and some of the issues of which you will need to be aware. You can keep up to date with these developments by reading one of the vast range of Internet-related magazines or by searching for more information on the Internet. Chapter 12 includes details of some useful Web sites.

Internet access via your fridge!

At some point in the near to medium future, most household appliances – ranging from your fridge to each light switch – will have Internet access. This does not necessarily mean that you will use your fridge to surf the Web, but it does mean that the fridge will be capable of connecting to the Internet and will be accessible from the Web. In theory this means that if you were away from home you would be able to use your mobile phone (with Internet access) to switch on your hallway light from halfway across the world, making your house look 'lived in'.

Another application might be to install a small video camera (some of which now cost as little as £30) connected to the Internet in your home. This would enable you to monitor your house remotely. This has commercial uses as well. For example, potential customers (this is already in existence on some Web sites) could get a feel for the ambience in a restaurant before they commit themselves to making a booking.

Similarly, your fridge might have Internet access, not necessarily for you to surf the Web, but for very specific applications such as recipe retrieval or ordering replacement items from an online grocery store. All you will need to do is use a built-in bar code scanner to scan the empty orange juice carton before you throw it away, creating an online shopping list for when you are ready to receive your next grocery delivery.

Bluetooth Wireless

To access the Internet, you currently need a computer and telephone line or an interactive digital television. Named after a 10th-century Danish king who united most of Scandinavia, Bluetooth aims to change that and get rid of the mass of wires which are currently necessary. Bluetooth is a new networking standard, which uses VHF radio waves (on the same frequency as baby monitors and microwaves) to transmit voices and data between electronic devices without the need for cables. Bluetooth is supported by a consortium of companies which includes Intel, Motorola, Toshiba, Siemens and Microsoft.

A practical use of Bluetooth technology is the ability to use wireless ordering systems such as those currently used in some restaurants, whereby your waiter keys your order into a PDA (Personal Digital Assistant) and it is transmitted straight to the kitchen.

Other uses will relate to provision of information 'on the run'. A Bluetooth device placed in a mobile phone or notebook PC has what is called a 'service discovery protocol'. In effect, it looks for other Bluetooth devices within a 10-metre range and automatically works out whether it can share information. Current research is trying to extend the range of Bluetooth devices to 100 metres and beyond.

This will mean that relevant information can be served up to your phone or PDA at any time.

Personal Digital Assistants (PDAs)

PDAs are rapidly growing in popularity and include devices such as the Palm Pilot or Psion Revo. They were originally conceived as small digital diaries, allowing users to carry their agenda and address book with them, with automatic synchronization with personal or desktop computers.

This is still their primary use today, but because they are built on a 'computer platform', many other uses are being developed for them. For example, you can now buy a small mobile phone that connects directly into the expansion slot of the PDA so that one device will then contain a telephone, address book and diary. Because PDAs typically have larger screens than mobile phones, they are easier to use to access the Internet (via the mobile phone extension) than WAP services.

Numerous Web sites have anticipated this feature and have developed information services that can be downloaded via the PC directly into the PDA. Two examples of these are US companies Vindigo and Avantgo. Both have acquired a vast amount of city-specific information, which is constantly updated and can be downloaded directly into the PDA.

Vindigo have formed a partnership with the London Evening Standard newspaper's Web site, www.thisislondon.co.uk. As a result, once the information is downloaded to the PDA, the user has instant access to restaurant, shopping, cinema and nightlife reviews, and information that they can carry with them free of charge. Avantgo and Vindigo make money through advertising revenue, so if users were to look up a film near Leicester Square, they might also see an advertisement for a restaurant near the cinema.

Simple Message Service (SMS)

Several years ago, when the current GSM mobile system was being developed, a forward-thinking engineer suggested that a Simple Message Service (SMS) should be included as part of the specification. This meant that every single mobile phone built could automatically be used to send text messages of up to 160 characters.

This feature was not very widely used at first, but people suddenly started to realize they could often send a message in lieu of making a phone call.

Scoot, a form of online 'yellow pages' in the United Kingdom, have perfected the use of SMS. If for example you are in your car and phone them up asking for a restaurant recommendation for the town you are driving to, they will send the name, address and phone number of the restaurant directly to your mobile phone via SMS, so you do not have to look for a pen and paper while driving.

Among the largest segments of users are children and teenagers who send each other SMS messages via their mobile phones, often combining symbols together in what are called 'emoticons'; for example, :-) denotes a happy face or :-(for a sad face. Advertisers and marketers are now starting to take advantage of this development to promote to quite precise market segments.

Wireless Application Protocol (WAP)

A more recent development stems from a perceived desire to access the Internet directly from mobile phones. Since there was no standard way to do this, a group of the leading mobile phone companies, including Nokia, Ericsson and Motorola, got together and developed the Wireless Application Protocol (WAP).

This has not yet been as successful as anticipated. One reason is that many existing mobile phone owners will probably need to buy a new device that supports the WAP standard, and even then many Web sites that can be viewed on a PC are impossible to view on a small mobile phone screen. Web site owners therefore have to decide whether they need to develop specific sites for WAP users, as some sites like Yahoo! have done.

In order to access the Internet, it is also necessary to 'connect' to a WAP site first, which takes time and costs money, often at premium rates.

Success of iMode in Japan

The Japanese have developed their own version of WAP, called iMode, which is already very popular. Its success is partly due to the fact that it is not necessary to connect specifically to the iMode service because phones are already always connected to it. There are also hundreds of thousands of iMode-developed sites in Japan, offering everything from online banking to dating services (these are the most popular!).

Thousands of people are subscribing to iMode every day and there are almost 16 million users in Japan. NTT DoCoMo, the company offering iMode in Japan, is now considering bringing it over to Europe, where it may be more successful than WAP.

Location-sensitive marketing

Many companies are already using 'location-sensitive marketing' to promote to carefully defined target markets by mobile phone.

This could mean sending an audio advertisement to mobile-phone users within a specific geographic area to tell them that a nearby hotel or bar is having a happy hour or special promotion. In Singapore, films have been promoted used WAP, using a 10-second audio clip to promote a film and then offering users the chance to buy cinema tickets through their phones.

A free service called '((!)) ZagMe' has been launched which sends shopping-related messages directly to mobile-phone users. Users register on the ((!)) ZagMe Web site or by telephone, detailing their preferences so that special offers can be 'zagged' to them. The registration process includes profiling information, and also gives ZagMe users the opportunity to specify what kind of offers they are not interested in.

This kind of 'location-sensitive marketing' has been successfully tested at Lakeside shopping centre in Essex. Once they had entered the shopping centre and registered to use the service, specifying their likes and dislikes, users were targeted with relevant messages. The service was used in a variety of ways, such as the promotion of opening offers at new shops by offering freebies to the first 100 people to go straight to the store, and for time-specific offers. The latter was particularly useful for food outlets wishing to sell surplus food before they closed.

Interactive Digital Television (iDTV)

Interactive Digital Television (iDTV) allows viewers to sit at home and interact with their TV sets, whether by having a greater choice of viewing options or by accessing the Internet.

If it works as envisaged, iDTV is likely to have a major impact on the profiles and attitudes of people using the Internet, particularly in terms of e-commerce. A major survey in 2000 found that almost half of all consumers would prefer to shop on the Internet via their iDTV, compared with just a quarter who said they would prefer to do it on their computer.

This is apparently because viewers tend to watch television in a 'lean back', relaxed mode, using their iDTV for entertainment and using a remote control or an infra-red keyboard for navigation. This contrasts with a 'lean forward' mode when they use a PC or laptop, with a mouse for navigation. Research from the Henley Centre suggests people associate the television set with quality time, while Internet usage via a PC is far more strongly associated with work. As use of iDTV builds, this is likely to have a profound effect on bookings for leisure and holiday products and services.

Teletext is already a success story in terms of selling travel and other products, although it does not allow direct booking. The success of teletext is nonetheless good news for iDTV as it proves that people will sit at home and book holidays just by scrolling through often-tedious pages of text information on their television. If they are prepared to do this, then they must surely be more than willing to buy similar products when they are able to use a much more visual and interactive system.

There are currently some disadvantages to accessing the Internet via iDTV. It can be slow because of limited bandwidth, and because television sets have a lower resolution than PC screens, it can be difficult to read Web sites. This means that Web sites that are intended to be viewed on iDTV will need to be redesigned with larger size text and images. In the future, more and more homes will be connected to very high bandwidth Internet connections that will enable the delivery of a high-definition screen image with much improved sound quality, enabling viewers to watch videos-on-demand, by downloading them in real time from the Internet.

Screen or Web phones

As mentioned earlier, the Internet will soon be built into many everyday devices. In addition to the television, a very likely candidate is the telephone. The idea is straightforward: take a telephone, add a screen, keyboard and modem and you have a simple device that can be used to access the Internet for simple tasks such as buying a book or online banking.

Such devices are likely to be used by people who already use the Internet at work but who do not have a PC at home, as well as people who are new to the Internet and who do not want to use a PC. Several companies are working on the development of screen phones and some of them are already available to buy today.

Speech-operated surfing

Companies such as SpeechWorks are now pioneering technology which enables people to access the Internet using conventional telephones and to 'voice surf'. The speech browser will encourage even people who do not want to use a PC or television to get online, as well as offering an alternative method of Internet access for existing users. The speech browser will transfer users from a portal to other speech-enabled sites. It does this using a verbal equivalent of HTML links, the 'language' of the Internet.

The SpeechWorks technology is already being used by United Airlines and a New York restaurant information service. Users can telephone the service and listen to reviews and other information, or transfer to book a table. They do this without human intervention, but through digital 'Chef Bob', who asks callers simple questions to find out what kind of restaurant they might be interested in.

Smell the Internet

One of the reasons that the Internet has become so powerful so quickly is that it is interactive and capable of using different senses. Sites already use text and pictures, sound and video to make an impact. In the future, it is possible they will also use another sense – scent.

A US-based company, DigiScents, is now working on what it calls 'iSmell digital scent technology' and getting ready to launch the first scent-enabled portal, called a 'Snortal'! DigiScents analyses smells according to their chemical composition and then converts them into special files which can be combined with Web content. In order to access scent-enabled sites, users will need to buy a small add-on for their computer which is about the size of a small speaker and which will 'unpack' the smell using scent cartridges.

Faster access

It is not very long since jokes abounded about the World Wide Wait but faster access is now becoming a reality.

■ New computers are being routinely sold with 56k modems, much faster than the old 28.8k modems which many initial users had.

■ The price of ISDN lines is coming down. ISDN lines are digital and effectively guaranteed to be twice as fast as a 56K modem.

■ ADSL (Asynchronous Digital Subscriber Loop) is now available via mainstream operators such as BT and provides permanent, 24-hour Internet access, up to 10 times faster than current modem speeds.

■ Cable modems offer a similar service to ADSL through cable companies. There is increased competition between the telecommunications and cable companies, bringing prices down.

Micro-payments and e-wallets

Despite concerns about security issues, consumers are increasingly willing to buy goods and services online using their credit cards. However, they are currently unlikely to make much smaller payments by credit card for lower-value items like downloadable map guides or small bites of information.

New systems are now being introduced to make it easier to buy less expensive items without using a credit card. Methods vary from adding the payment to telephone bills to using pre-paid shopping vouchers that can be topped up like pre-pay mobile phone-cards.

2

UNDERSTANDING INTERNET USERS

The profile of Internet users is changing. Five years ago young geeks were more likely than grannies to be using the Internet. Nowadays, retired people make up a significant proportion of Internet users and are one of the fastest growing segments of the market. This chapter looks at the changing profile of Internet users in the United Kingdom and overseas.

HOW INTERNET USAGE IS MEASURED

As the medium becomes increasingly sophisticated, there are more and more companies like Jupiter MMXI and Forrester springing up to profile users and develop data on their habits. Estimated current and projected Internet usage figures vary widely according to the different research companies. They all have slightly different methods of gathering their data.

NetValue and Jupiter MMXI work with panels of carefully selected Web users. The aim of the selection process is to ensure that participants are representative of the Web community as a whole. The selected panellists are issued with software that tracks their every move online.

NetPoll uses a mix of online and offline market research techniques to chart the attitudes and behaviour of Internet users.

Forrester's quarterly *Internet User Monitor* takes a different approach. In addition to offline market research, the company conducts online polls on around 150 sites. These are multiple-choice questionnaires and aimed at establishing who users are, what they do on the Web and what they think about the available services.

Such companies can only give an indication of who is online and what they are looking for, but their research reports are a useful starting point. In such a fast-moving environment, it is inevitable that the profile of Internet users will change. The following pages give a brief insight into the profile of Internet users at the beginning of 2001. Chapter 12 gives details of Web sites and other sources of detailed data and current statistics about Internet users to bring you up to date.

INTERNET USAGE IN THE UNITED KINGDOM

The following figures show details of Internet usage according to a selection of studies and surveys.

Total number of Internet users (at home, work and college) in the United Kingdom

Forrester (end 2000)	18.80m
e-Mori (June 2000)	13.40m
Nielsen NetRatings (November 2000)	19.98m

Number of home Internet users in the United Kingdom

Forrester (end 2000)	13.00m
e-Mori (June 2000)	10.40m
Nielsen NetRatings (April 2000)	8.30m

It is estimated that in the 12 months up to the beginning of 2001, UK home Internet use increased by around a third. Jupiter MMXI predicts that the number of people online at home, work and university in the United Kingdom will grow by almost 40 per cent in 2001. BRMB Interactive's study in 2001 indicates that around 80 per cent of Internet users access the Web at home, around 38 per cent at work and about 18 per cent at school or university.

It could be argued that there is some double-counting if one considers the number of Internet users at home, work and college. However, recent research seems to indicate that the reasons for use vary at home and work, so the same user may have a completely different usage (and buying) profile in the two different locations.

Internet population by gender (% of male/female users)

United Kingdom	60/40
France	61/39
Spain	71/29
Germany	62/38
Sweden	55/45
United States	52/48

Source: *Net Value/Net Profit* 2001

Although there are more men online than women, the balance is shifting to become more even. This is important for the tourism industry because women make the majority of decisions about holiday bookings. In countries such as Scandinavia and the United States, where Internet use is more established, the proportion of male/female users is already much more even.

Age of Internet users

15–24	22%
25–34	27%
35–44	23%
45–54	16%
55+	12%

Source: *e-MORI* June 2000

The age profile of Internet users is changing, with increasingly heavy usage by older people. This is the fastest growing sector of Internet usage. It is a particularly important segment for the tourism and leisure industry as people aged 45+ have increased leisure time and higher disposable income, with a greater propensity to spend their money on travel and other leisure experiences.

Socio-economic background of Web users

AB	38%
C1	34%
C2	12%
DE	12%

Source: *e-MORI* June 2000. Note: the percentages do not add up to 100% because of rounding errors.

Usage is still weighted towards more affluent people, but increased access via different devices such as mobile phones and interactive digital television is likely to even out the socio-economic profile of users.

KEY FACTS

The following is a selection of pertinent facts and figures from a wide variety of research sources.

■ The United Kingdom still lags well behind the United States where, according to the figures published by NetValue, almost 50 per cent of households are online. The same report found that 25 per cent of Britain's online community had been online for six months or less, compared with 15.1 per cent in the United States.

■ Not surprisingly, new users are on average less likely to carry out transactions online than veterans. Experienced users – those with connections dating back to 1997 or earlier – currently account for 80 per cent of all Web commerce.

■ When first buying something online, most people start with a low-value item such as a book or CD to minimize risk, before moving on to other goods and services. Holiday flights are already popular purchases, so it is likely that booking other leisure-related products and services online will become equally prevalent.

▓ Women's online behaviour patterns differ from those of their male counterparts. Men tend to like computer and sports sites, and visit a lot more sites overall. Women tend to focus on a smaller number of sites, particularly those relating to information, community and retailing.

▓ Children tend to use the net to access games and entertainment-orientated sites but there is a growing awareness of the medium's educational importance. An increasing proportion of school-age children say they use the Internet to help them with their homework. A recent survey showed that in the United States 96 per cent of 6–12-year-olds have accessed the Internet at some point, and average time spent on the Internet each week is as high as 5.5 hours.

▓ Research in 2000 seemed to indicate that the Internet population is well educated. Students accounted for around 19.9 per cent of the Web population. People educated to degree level made up 20 per cent of Internet users. Those with A-levels accounted for about 19 per cent. At the other end of the educational spectrum, only 5 per cent had no qualifications at all.

▓ In their April 2000 report, Forrester asked whether respondents had made any of the following purchases in recent months: 54 per cent of respondents had bought a mobile phone, 50 per cent had booked a foreign holiday and 41 per cent had bought a computer. The same survey found that while only 38 per cent of net users have actually made an online purchase, large numbers use the Web to research goods and services that they might buy at a later date.

▓ The trend is towards growth, with around 50 per cent of respondents saying they expected to buy music online over the next six months and 48 per cent indicating they might well purchase holidays.

INTERNET ACCESS WORLDWIDE

The following gives a brief overview of Internet usage worldwide.

Internet use as a percentage of the population

United Kingdom	33.3
France	15.6
Spain	11.7
Germany	20.8
Sweden	56.8
United States	54.3

Source: *Net Profit* February 2001

Online shoppers (% of Internet users)

United Kingdom	37
France	13
Spain	7
Germany	31
Sweden	31
United States	19

Source: *eRatings* mid-2000

France

Internet usage in France appears to be surprisingly low. This is mainly due to the legacy of Minitel, a text-based information system introduced by France Telecom in 1982, with simple low-speed terminals connected to the France Telecom network. They were initially intended to replace phone books and to allow access to information services. An estimated 25 million people (almost half the French population) now use the Minitel terminals in homes and offices to buy train tickets, check stocks, search databases, access news and directories, publish classified ads and enter chat rooms.

Each year these activities are worth around 2 billion euros. Minitel users have to pay to access the service. They are charged premium telephone rates on a per-minute basis and receive their invoice with the telephone bill. The success of Minitel has shown that the French are definitely prepared to use a similar system to the Internet, and French Minitel users are now slowly moving over to the Internet itself, enticed by lower charges and broader Web site content. France is quickly adopting digital TV, bringing interactive services to non-PC-owning households.

Germany

The Germans are set to dominate Europe in terms of e-commerce. MMXI Jupiter expects that by 2004 Germany will account for 26 per cent of Western European e-commerce, with the United Kingdom at 18 per cent and France lagging behind at 13 per cent. This is an interesting statistic since German shoppers are uneasy about completing transactions over the Internet. Research by Jupiter showed that 45 per cent of German online consumers have reservations about using a credit card to make purchases, while only 29 per cent of UK shoppers showed a similar reluctance. Germans are more likely to research online and then phone through a booking.

Other markets

Scandinavia has benefited from a liberal telecommunications infrastructure and a real need to communicate. The Internet is seen as one way to keep in touch when the roads are closed in winter.

The time spent online varies from country to country. AOL (America Online) users in the United States now average 30 hours a month online, while Freeserve users in the UK average only 10 hours. The figures are similar for the rest of Europe including Scandinavia. The main reason is that in Europe telephone charges are based on metered rates while United States users benefit from flat rates.

In other world markets, Internet usage also looks set to escalate. Out of Japan's population of around 120 million people, approximately 27 million had an Internet connection in August 2000, according to the Japanese Ministry of Post and Telecommunications (MPT). By March 2001 the number had risen dramatically, but the majority of Internet connections are via mobile phones rather than PCs. In March 2001 there were over 30 million subscribers to mobile Internet services.

Japan has its own very popular wireless Internet service called iMode. The MPT estimates that by 2005, 80 million Japanese will have access to a Web-enabled mobile phone.

Australia is following the US and European models. PC penetration is high at around 50 per cent, and around 28 per cent of the total population have Internet access at home.

China currently has an online population of only around 15.8 million people, but this figure is growing rapidly. Jupiter MMXI predicts that the Middle East will have a compound annual growth rate of 59 per cent in the period between 1999 and 2005, and Latin America and Eastern Europe will have growth of around 35 per cent each. One likely development is that growth will be accelerated by investment from global companies who are keen to enter these important markets.

SEGMENTING THE INTERNET MARKETPLACE

Just as marketers divide other consumer groups into manageable clusters and name them according to their characteristics and buying behaviour, various organizations are now trying to identify specific types of Internet users according to their lifestyle and demographic profile.

CACI Information Solutions define five user groups, which they call 'eTypes'. eTypes is their targeting tool for understanding consumer online behaviour. Constructed using CACI's core demographic and lifestyle datasets, combined with Fletcher Research data, eTypes provides a way of knowing more about people on the Internet, describing their Internet usage and their likely lifestyle profile. The information is updated every six months.

CACI Ltd suggests several ways of using the eTypes information.

Online

An eTypes analysis indicates the profile of people as they register at a Web site. This means that since Webmasters will know more about overall Internet experience and usage patterns, they will be able to forecast the potential for e-commerce. Such profiles can also be used to help plan Web site developments to match the confidence levels of users.

For example, if you find that your site users are mainly 'virtual virgins' you will need to give them more care and guidance than if they are 'surfing suits'.

At its most sophisticated, this profiling can be extended to give recognition of customers at registration, enabling implementation of appropriate personalization strategies.

Offline

ETypes allows targeting for direct mail based on users' behaviour online. A company that wants to build traffic to its Web site can use names and addresses of people in their target market. It also means that the company can build a target market by combining likely Internet usage with lifestyle profiles and product preferences.

Alternatively, eTypes can help to analyse existing customer databases to identify those most likely to use online facilities. This helps companies either to target those customers most likely to be responsive or to assess the longer-term potential of the Internet for their business.

The five stages of 'eTypes' according to CACI Ltd

Stage 1: virtual virgins

These people are those least likely to have purchased online. Fewer than two in a thousand will have made any form of online purchase in the last month. Their time online is half the national average and they are likely to have started using the Internet more recently than other people.

With the exception of using chat rooms, these people do Internet activities less frequently than average. Because of their relative inexperience, they are more likely to worry about security and delivery problems when buying online, and to consider the process to be complicated.

People in this group are twice as likely to be female compared to any other group. The elderly and children are more commonly found in this type than any other.

Stage 2: chatters and gamers

These people, predominately young males, might spend as much time online as the most avid type of Internet user. However, they tend not to be buyers and only one in five will ever have made an online purchase. They may consider shopping online to be difficult and their fear of delivery and security problems is above average.

These people are keen 'chatters and gamers' who use news groups and download as frequently as the most active and experienced surfers.

Nearly half these people are aged under 25. The school-children in this type are more likely to connect from school/ university than any other type, although connection from home is still most frequent.

Stage 3: dot.com dabblers

As average Internet users, these people have mixed feelings regarding the pros and cons of online shopping. Around 40 per cent will have made some form of purchase online and, with the exception of chatting, their interests spread all forms of Internet activity.

These people may value the Internet for convenience and speed of delivery. Alternatively, a specialist product not available elsewhere may have introduced them to buying online. In any event, their enthusiasm for e-commerce is not yet complete.

Stage 4: surfing suits

Although they spend less time on the Internet than average, these people can be quite enthusiastic online purchasers. They are more likely than most to have bought books, software, hardware, holidays, groceries, insurance and tickets for events online.

Shopping online is seen to offer benefits such as a range of product information, speed of ordering, price advantages and an element of fun. The usual e-commerce fears are less likely to concern these people.

They control their time on the Internet and surfing, searching, and tend to prefer e-mail and news groups rather than chat, games or magazines.

Stage 5: wired living

These are cosmopolitan young people and the most extensive Internet users, spending about four and a half hours online each week. They are more experienced than most online users and on average have been using the Internet for three years. Over 70 per cent will have purchased over the Internet, covering between them the full gamut of products available for purchase. Over 60 per cent are educated to degree level.

These people use the Web as part of their lifestyle. Preferred interests tend to be newsgroups, news and magazines, with only an average interest in games or chat.

Further information about the eTypes is available on the Web site www.caci.co.uk.

IMPORTANCE OF THE INTERNET FOR THE TOURISM AND HOSPITALITY INDUSTRY

The Internet lends itself to online promotion and sales of some products and services better than others. Tourism, leisure and hospitality are particularly popular. They are information-intensive services which consumers enjoy researching online and, because they tend to be quite expensive, buyers find the Internet a useful medium for comparing prices.

Many consumers experiment with online purchasing by first of all buying small, low-cost items like books and CDs. They then go on to make other purchases which are usually either holidays and flights or computer goods. The percentage of purchasers of entertainment, holiday and leisure-related products is already quite significant, as shown by a *Which?* Online survey in 2000.

Products bought online by UK Web users

Books	23%
CDs/videos	19%
Flights/holidays	19%
Computer goods	19%

Film/theatre tickets	10%
Financial services	8%
Groceries	6%
Other	4%

Just as books, holidays and leisure services are usually bought without experiencing them first, so buying them online is not so different from the offline experience. More tangible products such as clothes, which consumers prefer to try on and touch, have not yet become such popular items for e-commerce.

In terms of online activity, tourism is a major growth area as various reports have shown. A Forrester survey in April 2000 found that around 48 per cent respondents said they were likely to purchase holidays online in the future.

In January 2001, the Internet travel intelligence company Phocuswright released the *European Online Travel Marketplace 2000–2002* report, which predicted that the European online travel market will soar from US $2.9 billion in 2000 to US $10.9 billion in 2002, nearly a 300 per cent two-year gain.

It suggested that factors contributing to this growth are: increased usage of the Internet and WAP phones; the breakdown of e-commerce barriers such as bill payment, security and privacy concerns; improved telecommunications; and the influx of new and improved online travel services.

Companies such as Expedia.com, Travelocity.com and Lastminute.com have begun to build significant market share and, at the same time, they are raising public awareness of travel e-commerce. One of the great advantages of the Internet is its global reach, which is particularly important and relevant for the tourism industry.

The Phocuswright report found that airline Web sites and tour operators controlled 28 per cent and 27 per cent respectively of the European online travel market in 2000. Online travel agencies had a 26 per cent market share, railways 9 per cent, hotels 7 per cent and car rental companies 3 per cent.

The *Internet European Travel Monitor* published by etourism newsletter.com in July 2000 found that a total of 16.9 million international trips by Europeans were initiated on the Internet in 1999. Almost a quarter of these trips were also booked and paid for online. Most of them were for leisure purposes.

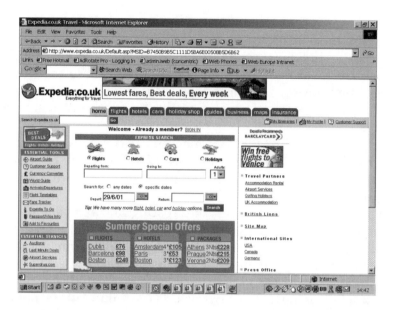

Figure 3.1 Companies such as Expedia and Travelocity are responsible for raising awareness of travel e-commerce

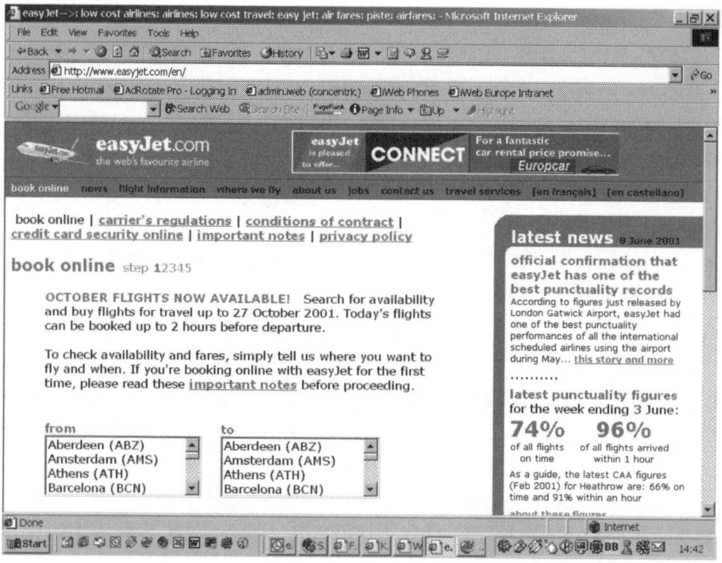

Figure 3.2 Easyjet: this low-cost airline already receives over 80 per cent of all bookings online

The same report also indicated the types of short breaks and holidays more likely to be booked online than offline. These were skiing holidays, travel to special events and city breaks. These are all growth areas and travellers in these categories have a high propensity for independent travel (as opposed to booking through travel agents), so this development is encouraging.

Interestingly, this survey found that British, Swedish and German Internet users were most likely to book online, as were more affluent, well-educated people aged 30–44 with young children.

This report is particularly interesting and relevant to the tourism industry because it had a greater sample size and broader perspective than most other surveys. Four hundred thousand people were interviewed in 33 countries.

A report from NOP in February 2001 suggested that in the four weeks leading up to Christmas 2000, around 480,000 people in the United Kingdom shopped online for holidays and travel, spending an average of £420 each.

Most of the big hotel chains now offer online booking but levels of use in 2000 seem to have been relatively low: only around 2–5 per cent of all bookings taken. Conservative estimates are that this figure will increase to around 15 per cent within five years. Sites such as www.smoothhound.com have been successful in helping smaller hotels and guesthouses to get online and benefit from the global reach of the Internet.

To date, simple transactions such as flight-only bookings have been leading the way in terms of e-commerce, but in the near future it is likely that it will be easier to book more complex tailor-made holidays online too.

The growth of the Internet has led to two opposing trends: first, the development of niche market products, and second, development of global brands. On the one hand, the Internet appears to favour global brands whose reach extends worldwide. There are numerous global alliances developing whose main priority is to build their brand and achieve a greater market share. However, the Internet has also been beneficial to smaller, niche operators.

The tourism and hospitality industries are incredibly fragmented, offering very diverse and complex products that are increasingly sought after by individual travellers. The Internet is now making it possible for small suppliers to bypass a long chain of intermediaries and to reach their target markets more directly. Niche products are favoured by a growing number of consumers who until now have been unable to find them in traditional High Street travel agencies.

The Internet is making it easier for people to pursue specialist sporting activities, find out where they can develop a new hobby or buy leisure-related products. The Internet lends itself well to collaborative marketing and a consortium approach so that consumers can find niche products and all the ingredients for tailor-made travel much more easily than ever before.

cPulse published its survey of 6,580 travel site users in late 2000. It found that the number of new users of niche travel sites was up over 80 per cent in late 2000 compared with the same time the previous year. Over 80 per cent of users of these sites said they would use them again.

The study showed that smaller sites targeting specific customer groups had a better chance of providing relevant content than sites that cater for mass audiences, with users believing the information provided on niche sites was more accurate.

BENEFITS OF THE INTERNET FOR TOURISM AND LEISURE

Tourism and leisure are ideal products and services for online distribution.

■ They are effectively 'virtual': you do not see or experience a holiday or football match before you buy your tickets. The purchase is made in advance, based on perceptions of the services and experience offered and in anticipation that it will be enjoyable.

■ Difficulties in delivery and fulfilment services have been cited as major reasons why some e-commerce sites fail. However, there is no physical delivery for most tourism and leisure products and services, so this is less likely to be a problem. It may be necessary to provide tickets but this can be arranged relatively easily. They can be posted or picked up from collection points. The 'ticketless' airlines such as Go and Easyjet generate customer reference numbers online and provide documents which can be printed off by the consumer.

■ Tourism is an information-rich product; we like to know quite a lot about our destination or the experience before we buy and it is actually easier to provide this information online than to train staff to know about all possible options. Staff in a travel agency or theatre box office cannot possibly know about all the places and plays for which they sell tickets, whereas the public can usually find most of the information they need (no matter how obscure) on the Internet.

■ Travel and leisure are often repeat purchases. When making repeat bookings, limited human intervention is required so consumers are increasingly content to buy online. This is particularly true for straightforward purchases like flight, sports or theatre tickets.

THE MANY BENEFITS TO PROMOTION ON THE INTERNET

Opportunity to sell at the last minute

Most tourism and leisure products are perishable. If a hotel does not sell its bedrooms on one particular night, it will never have the opportunity to recoup that lost revenue; event organizers only get one chance to sell each ticket or seat for a given performance or event. The Internet can make it easier to sell such products at the last minute, avoiding loss of revenue.

Currency of information

Web sites can include the most recent information available with frequent updates. We can use them to show latest availability, current weather reports, event updates and so on. Thus the Internet is the ideal way to communicate information at the last minute. For example, travellers can consult Web sites showing train timetables just before travelling, receiving information and updates about engineering works which might affect their journey time.

Fast reactions

Internet marketing allows Webmasters to react very quickly to changing market conditions; you can change prices, offers, information and so on according to demand, far more quickly than with any other promotional activity. If you make a special offer online, you can also remove the offer as soon as take-up has reached capacity levels. Consumers increasingly expect 'instant gratification'; the Internet facilitates this.

Promotion and sales outlet combined

Selling is usually at least a two-step process: first of all a product is promoted and then it is sold. These two steps normally take place at different locations and there is always the danger that a sale will be suspended between the two stages. The Internet combines and facilitates the process and means that one Web site can be used to promote and then sell to customers online.

Just a few years ago anyone wanting to book a hotel room would probably have requested a brochure, then either telephoned or written to the hotel to make a booking and then awaited a written confirmation. Now you can look for a hotel on the Internet and confirm a booking immediately by e-mail or online in real time, paying for it at the same time with a credit card.

A one-to-one marketing method

Traditional print material is viewed sequentially; readers flick through brochures to find details which are relevant to them. Information on the Internet is presented according to demand and relevant information can be directly requested, so it is more of a one-to-one marketing method. The Internet and e-mails are viewed on a screen right in front of the user, so it is a very personal means of communication.

Most people are passionate about their holidays and leisure time, with very personal likes and dislikes, so the opportunity to communicate with them, in such a direct way and taking account of their preferences, is powerful. Web sites can also be customized or personalized according to users' needs.

Greater market segmentation

Marketers recognize the need for market segmentation and spend a significant proportion of their budget and time trying to break down their target markets into cluster groups. However, they often fail to find ways of using this information when developing promotional activities.

The Internet makes it much easier to target different market segments, offering different types of information or services according to the profiles of users. It is also useful for organizations with a dominant corporate identity or brand that wish to target audiences who might not react positively to that identity. Such companies can build micro- or sub-sites which communicate a different message to their main site, without damaging their brand.

Opportunity for 'mood marketing'

Until recently most market segmentation techniques have relied on determining whom to target, building a picture of people according to their age, background, job, where they live and so on.

These factors have an impact on our leisure and holiday choices but are unlikely to be such strong determinants as other aspects such as whom we want to enjoy our leisure time with; how much time we have; our need for relaxation at certain times and self-development at others. Although the person we are targeting remains the same age as before, with the same background, income and so forth, their decisions change according to these powerful determining factors.

The Internet offers us the opportunity to segment much more carefully and to promote according to mood. Rather than simply presenting information in a listings or directory-style format (as with traditional print), it is possible to offer information which is sorted according to themes and motivations or personal situations. This means that the consumer does not have to scan through tedious lists of hotels searching for pertinent phrases like 'relaxing, quiet location – come and be pampered' but instead asks for information about a relaxing break rather than an active one, so that only relevant information comes on screen.

Open all hours

Unlike most businesses, the Internet can be accessed 24 hours a day, 365 days a year, offering constant information and extending marketplaces.

Interactive means more memorable

The interactive nature of the Internet means there is potential to make a much greater impact than with traditional print media – we remember 10 per cent of what we read, 30 per cent of what we see, 50 per cent of what we see and hear, 90 per cent of what we see, hear and do. The Internet is a multi-media experience, with the capacity to present information through text, graphics, sound and video. It is interactive; every time a user wants information, they 'click' to receive it.

Reduced costs

The Internet enables faster communication at a fraction of the price of traditional media. Organizations such as tourist information centres spend a high proportion of their promotional budgets on producing and distributing information in response to fairly standard enquiries and frequently asked questions. Now when someone telephones to request a brochure or other information, the centre can simply refer the enquirer to a Web site, removing the need to send out print material. This not only saves costs but also offers an instant response, satisfying enquirers and increasing conversions of enquiries into firm bookings.

Another way of reducing costs is to use e-mail instead of traditional direct mail. It offers the opportunity to send out mailshots directly to a carefully targeted list of people at a very low cost, and has the added advantage that e-mails will arrive right in front of the recipient's eyes on their computer screen.

Easy to monitor effectiveness

The Internet is one of the most measurable promotional methods. Technology allows us to track customers when they visit a site, assess how long they are spending in each of its areas, and trace these patterns whenever they visit the site again. If we were to compare this with traditional direct mail, it would be like knowing whether a potential customer had opened the envelope you posted to them, which paragraphs they read and which inserts they put in the bin, as well as knowing whether they open any future mailings you send them. You can also find out how users heard about your site without having to ask them, by simply interpreting site log files.

Customer profiling

The Internet offers a great opportunity to build a profile of users. At present user profiles seem to be built according to demographic details (location, age, socio-economics etc) rather than their behaviour on the Web. However, in the near future there will be more interpretation of buyer behaviour. Sites will become more intuitive and take advantage of opportunities to cross-sell. For example, it is possible to know if a user has visited a general site about Spain and then checked out flights to Spain on British Airways; in that case, they can then be presented with information about accommodation in Spain as well.

Collaboration made easier

Collaborative or consortia marketing is popular among tourism businesses. It offers an opportunity to share costs and build an umbrella identity or brand. However, when brochures and traditional print material are used, there is rarely space for each individual business or area to have more than a small presence and their identity is subsumed under the overall brand.

Collaborative marketing works particularly well on the Internet because a Web site can act as an umbrella marketing tool, but still allow individual businesses to retain their own strong identity by offering a link to their own site, or a micro-site.

Easy to use for market research

Traditional market research can be expensive due to the time taken to collect and process the results. The Internet and e-mail can be used to cut costs and increase response rates. To conduct market research you can either set up online forms or send out and collect questionnaires by e-mail, which dramatically reduces the cost and time taken to send out questionnaires. Since recipients only need to hit the 'reply' button to complete the questionnaires, response rates can be much higher than usual, especially if you offer an incentive. This is partly thanks to the immediacy of the medium and partly because respondents do not need to remember to post completed survey forms.

A one-stop shop for information

Good sites offer consumers a one-stop shop, providing all the related information they could possibly want, in just one place. They either make use of a whole network of links to other appropriate sites or are 'portals', grouping information together under an umbrella site.

Small suppliers are potentially as powerful as big ones

A Web site belonging to a small leisure operator can appear as substantial as that of a much larger company and in theory they both have an equal opportunity to promote themselves. This is good for small suppliers and their consumers. Niche operators and small businesses can now present themselves to a wider audience than ever before, at a fraction of the cost of traditional promotional methods.

TRENDS IN TOURISM AND LEISURE

This chapter looks at some of the most important consumer trends in tourism and leisure and their likely impact on Internet usage.

CONFLICTING TRENDS

Two conflicting trends are emerging connected with our leisure time. There is a polarization in terms of the amount of time different groups of people have. Some people such as those who are retired have more leisure time than ever before, whereas others such as young professionals have far less.

Implications of an ageing population

Over the last 50 years or so, most people have benefited from not only longer holiday entitlements and shorter working weeks but also shorter working lives. People who have already retired are likely to live longer and have higher disposable income than their counterparts several years ago.

Over the next 10 years there will be a large increase in the number of people in Britain aged 65 or over. By the year 2015 they will outnumber the under-16s for the first time in history. This is good news for tourism as the over-50s are a significant market segment. The older population is likely to be more active and have better health and higher disposable income than previous generations. They want to travel and enjoy their leisure time. Many of these people are experienced travellers, looking for increasingly exotic or interesting destinations, and they have high quality expectations. Over time they will become less likely to book packages and will become more independent. Since an increasingly high proportion of Internet users are 'silver surfers', it is likely they will use the Internet to research information and book leisure products.

Emergence of the cash rich, time poor

In stark contrast to the over-50s, people such as full-time professionals are now working longer hours than ever before. Work pressure and job insecurity make them less likely to take long holidays but more likely to take a series of short breaks, so they are away from work for shorter periods of time. In some cases, employees do not even take their full holiday entitlement. The result is an increase in the number of people who are cash rich, but time poor.

Questioning the need for all work and no play

Other people are starting to challenge the need to just work and are increasingly looking at ways of increasing their leisure time, whether by 'down-sizing' or simply changing the way they operate. This might mean working from home to reduce the number of hours spent commuting or becoming self-employed to have more control over their working life. Their leisure time is increasingly important to them.

Increased demands on our leisure time

In addition to the need to balance work and leisure, there are greater demands on our time, with more choices and an ever-increasing range of retail outlets to shop in, hobbies to pursue, fitness centres to visit and so on. Tourism and leisure services are now competing with retail opportunities, self-development courses and 'get fit' campaigns.

RELATED DEVELOPMENTS IN THE LEISURE AND TOURISM MARKET

Increased number of short breaks

One of the results of these trends is the increased number of short breaks being taken. People with plenty of time and disposable income take them as additional holidays throughout the year, and people who are cash rich but time poor take them as alternatives to longer holidays.

Search for quality experiences

Taking shorter holidays can mean that people look for a more intensive, quality experience. There is a greater expectation of 'perfect moments' because long working hours and stress put more emphasis on precious leisure time.

Busy executives have limited time, so they want to ensure they get value for time as well as value for money, and are often willing to pay more to guarantee a better experience. Tourists need to have trust in operators, airlines and destinations, and are more likely to choose brands based on quality and reliability than price-driven ones.

Demand for unusual destinations, not too far away

There is added pressure to find destinations which are not too far away and will not lead to jet lag. Travellers are looking for places with good communication links, in case it is necessary for someone to get in touch. With the growth of mobile phones and other communication devices we feel an increased need to be permanently in contact, so it can be difficult to truly escape from work when there are voice-mail and e-mail messages to check.

Demand for self-discovery and chances to learn

There is an increased trend toward holidays and short breaks with a focus on some form of self-development or improvement. The Germans previously led the way in this market, with a marked turn away from purely sun–sea–sand holidays towards study tours during which they have an opportunity to learn something about the destination and culture. This does not mean that they have abandoned sun destinations, but that they also look for a more in-depth experience of the host country.

Some people choose short breaks as a chance to learn new skills or sample new activities. Activity holidays are therefore likely to increase in popularity.

This development will lead to increased segmentation of holiday motivations and different types of holiday. For example, we can already identify packages which focus on sports tourism, health spas and relaxation, food and drink, heritage and films.

Within this demand for new experiences and in a world of global brands, there is also a desire for authenticity. The opportunity to travel to a remote or smaller community is part of this, but so is the chance to put together one's own holiday and to deal directly with operators and hotels. The Internet is helping to drive this trend, because it offers greater direct access to a wider range of tourism and leisure suppliers.

Interest in sustainable tourism

Another important factor is greater interest in what destinations have to offer beyond basic tourism facilities. There is a growing awareness of the impact of visitors on host destinations, so people are recognizing the value of sustainable and ethical tourism. This means that visitors understand that tourism can have negative as well as positive effects and are becoming more interested in ensuring that their visit does not degrade the resources of the area they are visiting. Sustainable tourism does not adversely affect the environment or host community.

This awareness is likely to become stronger as travellers become better informed and more interested in the places they are visiting, rather than seeing them as simply somewhere which offers the right climate at the right price. Travellers interested in sustainable tourism spend more time researching their holiday choices, often asking questions which standard High Street travel agents cannot answer. They are increasingly turning to the Internet as a source of more detailed and direct information.

Growth of independent travel

One of the most dramatic changes in tourism has been the increase in independent-holiday-taking. Many people will continue to book packages with established tour operators but others, as they become more confident and adventurous, will make their travel arrangements directly with airlines and hotels, instead of turning to High Street travel agents.

As consumers realize that they have more choice and can secure better prices by booking directly – either by phone, teletext or the Internet – direct booking will certainly increase. There is demand for transparent value: while people are prepared to pay top price for top quality, they like to see what they are getting. They want to know what is involved and avoid paying middlemen, driving the trend to book directly – inevitably online.

Using the Internet to research and book holiday and leisure activities

Demand for short breaks and more adventurous or activity holidays is partly satisfied by a number of new Web sites, offering a wider choice and variety of destinations and activities than most High Street travel agencies. Recent research bears out this trend: many of the holidays booked online are short breaks.

Short breaks to unusual and 'green' destinations and activity breaks are 'information rich'. Most High Street travel agents are unable to service the demand for them fully, and certainly lack the product knowledge. The only tour operators' brochures racked by the majority of travel agents tend to be mainstream, so travellers are increasingly turning to the Internet as a source of information and then booking online.

Some of the hunger for short breaks has been fuelled by the growth of low-cost airlines like Easyjet, Ryanair and Go. Other people have been stimulated to take more short breaks through promotions by online companies like Lastminute.com.

Young professionals and other busy people are increasingly using the Internet as a way of finding quick solutions to their leisure-time needs. The times when they work and play are changing. They find that they need to take work home with them in the evening and then to organize their social life at work. The lunch hour is an ideal opportunity for sorting out their social life or holiday plans, with e-mail and the Internet the main way of doing this. The Henley Centre refer to this as 'homing at work'.

WAYS IN WHICH THE INTERNET IS CHANGING THE WAY WE LIVE

Price competition

Sites such as www.kelkoo.com have been developed specifically to make price comparisons easier for consumers. At present most of these deal with tangible, homogeneous products such as fridges or bicycles, but they will soon expand to cover a wider variety of services. Auction sites like QXL.com and Priceline. com already cover tourism and leisure services.

Even without sites dedicated to making price comparisons, Web users can easily compare prices and buy products from different suppliers in different countries, leading to greater price competition.

Better-informed customers and the changing role of sales people

Consumers are now able to undertake extensive research on the Internet before going to the shops to make a purchase. Sales people are increasingly seen as purchase facilitators or order-takers rather than advisors. Consumers may now feel they are better informed than ever before, becoming more powerful and in a stronger buying position.

Changing perceptions of 'service'

E-mail in particular has changed the speed at which we do business. Someone sends you a question by e-mail in the morning and, because it is so easy and quick to respond, expects to have an answer by the afternoon. When correspondence was by letter, this process used to take several days. As consumers, we also expect the pace of service to be faster than ever before.

We increasingly want to deal direct with suppliers. In 1992 1 per cent of all TV advertisements offered an 0800 number; now it is 20 per cent, making it easier for consumers to respond immediately. Consumers can now deal directly and easily with suppliers even when they are in different parts of the world or in different time zones.

It was initially believed that the Internet would help to cut the costs of customer service, removing the need for human intervention, but this has not been the case. Technology has acted as an enabler but has not been a complete solution. Web sites provide initial information and help to qualify sales but many consumers still want to speak to a 'real person'.

It is likely that in the near future voice-automated responses (using special technology which recognizes and responds to key words and phrases) will answer up to 40 per cent of all calls to call centres. This will leave 'live' staff free to respond to more complex enquiries.

Changing distribution channels – no middlemen

Although some people still prefer to speak to a human voice, many know exactly what they want and are content to make bookings and purchases online without any additional intervention, and without dealing with sales agents and middlemen.

The low-cost, no-frills airline Easyjet has been particularly successful in exploiting this development, giving a small discount incentive to encourage travellers to book online. Online bookings have developed rapidly and currently account for over 80 per cent of all Easyjet bookings.

The Internet can reduce the need for intermediaries such as travel agents. There have traditionally been several tiers of distribution between consumers and suppliers, and these may become redundant if the Internet provides a direct link between consumer and supplier. This process is known as 'disintermediation'. However, it can also be argued that what is actually happening is that new distributors and intermediaries such as Lastminute.com are simply springing up and taking a fresh approach.

6

DEVELOPING A MARKETING STRATEGY

Despite its strengths and benefits, the Internet should still be recognized as just one element of the overall marketing mix. It is one of several channels of communication and promotional tools which you can use to reach your customers. You will need to integrate your Web site into your overall marketing strategy, to enhance the value and effectiveness of both.

This chapter outlines the basic principles behind the development of a marketing strategy, helping you use the Internet as an effective promotional tool.

You will find a checklist for a marketing action plan at the end of this chapter.

KNOW YOUR PRODUCTS AND MARKETS

You will need to make sure you have a good overview of the current situation and how your business is running now, before going on to plan the future.

What's for sale? Who will buy it?

It is surprising how many business owners and managers do not have a clear idea of what they are selling, from a guest or visitor's perspective. When asked to describe what they sell, most people describe the physical characteristics of their products or components of a service. These are the *features*. But people do not buy features, they buy *benefits*. Most of us are selfish to some extent, so when we buy anything we implicitly ask ourselves the question, 'What's in it for me?' By describing the benefits of a product or service, you are effectively answering that question before it is even asked.

Let's take the example of Mr X who sells wooden garden furniture. He might describe it as 'reasonably priced, wooden chairs and tables', but what makes his customers buy his furniture?

They buy it because it makes their garden look more inviting, gives them somewhere to relax and unwind, or simply because their neighbours have some!

If Mr X shows photographs of happy-looking people using his furniture to relax in attractive settings, he will plant that idea in the minds of potential customers. They will forget that they do not have much time or that their garden does not look quite so good. Some will buy the furniture because in an ideal world, that is the lifestyle they want. Mr X has effectively imagined what his customers want and given it to them.

It is important to understand what the triggers are for your visitors, to provide the right sales messages and demonstrate that you can fulfil their needs. The way in which a product or service is 'positioned' is essential to its success.

Remember that successful products are often sold in a way that barely mentions their basic features, but instead stresses their benefits. Perfume is a good example of this. It is really just smelly water but perfume advertisers do not mention the scent, they promote romance and glamour, implying that if you wear the perfume you can have the same sort of lifestyle as the models in the advertisements.

Who are your current markets?

You are targeting human beings so you need to understand them.

▧ Humans are emotional; 85 per cent of all decisions are based on emotion, not logic.

▧ We are curious and like intrigue, romances and ongoing stories (hence the appeal of soaps on television).

▧ We want to make things better – for others and ourselves. We like advice; we seize on programmes, articles and training which might show us a better way of doing things, from home improvements to self-development.

▧ In many ways we do not really like change, yet we are always convinced the grass is greener on the other side so we keep looking anyway. It is probably *enforced* change we dislike, rather than change itself.

▧ Time is a major preoccupation; we complain of being short of time, we use it as an excuse and we love to find ways of saving time. We love labour-saving devices and solutions, even if we have to spend time working to pay for them! We consider ourselves to be busy and stressed, so potential time-saving solutions are often welcome – even at considerable expense.

▧ We have many fears and yet we continue to put ourselves into scary situations, constantly seeking challenges and new experiences, especially in our leisure time.

Reasons for buying any product or service

These are some of the main reasons why we buy anything:

▧ security;

▧ prestige;

▧ fun;

▧ fear;

▧ pride;

▧ ego;

■ ambition;

■ status;

■ desire.

Most of these reasons can be condensed into just two basic motivations:

■ Greed ('I need/want a new dress'), which includes not being left out, building our own self-image and even shopping to relieve boredom.

■ Fear (of the unknown, need for security for ourselves and loved ones), which is the way in which many insurance products are sold.

Motivations and influences

You should have a reasonable idea of who comes to visit your area or attraction, uses your services or books your accommodation. Before starting to develop new markets, it is a good idea to make sure you fully understand your current ones. Try to build on existing markets before you target totally new ones. Draw up a list of target markets by considering your current situation, asking yourself a range of questions.

■ Where do your customers come from and how far do they travel to get to you?

■ What is their average age and what is their 'life-stage'?

■ Who are they likely to be with when travelling, making bookings or buying from you? Are they couples, families, small groups of friends or colleagues, tour groups or whatever?

■ How would you describe their income group and lifestyle?

■ What are their interests?

■ Who/what influences their decisions?

■ How do they hear about you?

▨ Do they already use the Internet? What sort of activities do they use the Internet for? What types of sites do you think they use?

CONDUCT A SWOT ANALYSIS

A SWOT analysis is a useful way of assessing what you need to do to develop your business. It looks at the strengths, weaknesses, opportunities and threats. Strengths and weaknesses are usually internal issues, which you can control and change. Opportunities and threats are external factors over which you have less control. The marketing action plan at the end of this chapter includes some guidelines to help you conduct a SWOT analysis. This exercise will only be valuable to you if you think about how you can maximize the strengths and opportunities and what you will do to minimize the weaknesses and threats.

KNOW WHAT YOUR COMPETITORS ARE DOING

When you are involved in the day-to-day management of a business it is easy to think there is just not enough time to watch what your competitors are up to, but it does pay to do it. You can save time and money by keeping a keen eye on their activities, learning by their successes and failures.

You will need to find ways of differentiating yourself from your competition. Finding a competitive advantage means deciding how you can compete more effectively. This means offering your customers something which is better than your competitors' offer, either in real terms or through good marketing. You cannot do that unless you know what your competitors are doing.

The Internet is a great way to spy on your competition! You can find out as much as you want about them, anonymously. Look at your competitors' Web sites and consider their various aspects.

▨ What are your first impressions? Do they have a strong brand and identity?

■ Their pricing structure and how they present their prices; do they offer value for money?

■ How good is their marketing? Do you think they understand their customers?

■ Who do you think their customers are? Are their markets different to yours in any way?

You should be able to draw up a list of your closest competitors, looking at their prices, their welcome for visitors, facilities and promotional activities. Analyse each of these aspects and decide where you lag behind or are stronger. What are you going to do about it?

DEVELOP A COMPETITIVE ADVANTAGE

Every business needs a competitive advantage, or 'Unique Selling Point' (USP). This means thinking hard about what marks you out from your competitors and how you are really different. There are basically three ways of competing:

On price

Most people assume that competing on price means being the cheapest, but that is not necessarily so. Some businesses will succeed if they try to be the cheapest, but they need to be certain they can still make a profit and that their competitors are not going to undercut them. There is always a danger that someone will be cheaper. It can be dangerous to get caught in a downward price spiral.

Remember, too, that some people are very nervous of products or services which seem too cheap 'to be true'. If I suddenly announce to you that I am going to sell something at half its usual price, you are likely to be cynical and wonder 'what's the catch?'. I would need to work hard to convince you that it is a genuine offer, perhaps explaining why I can afford to sell it at half price.

Some businesses pride themselves on offering a far better service than their competitors and so their prices tend to be higher. Others create a perception of quality or prestige around more expensive goods (such as branded fashion goods) for which customers are willing to pay higher prices.

Do you remember the advertisements for Stella Artois beer – 'reassuringly expensive'? This beer is more expensive than other kinds and yet is one of the top-selling beers in Britain.

By being different

It is easier said than done, but anyone who can find a way of being slightly different from their competitors will avoid being in direct competition.

There are many ways of being different: offering a quirky or better product or service; having staff who are unusually friendly and helpful; different opening hours; or providing extended, more personalized services.

Some companies are considered different or better than others because of the way they present themselves, with a more professional image. In the tourism and leisure industry, *reputation* is often key to being different from other providers.

Perhaps more than any other industry, tourism is not one which just relies on individual components. Most tourism products are made up of several interrelated ingredients, which together deliver a total *experience*. A guesthouse may have the same number of bedrooms and basic services as its neighbour but be somehow made different by less tangible elements: the view from bedroom windows, pleasant garden, cosy lounge or warm welcome from the owners.

The basic elements of a tourism or leisure product may appear very similar but they can be brought together in different ways to develop an experience which is vastly different from competitors'. This could mean a quicker service, one which is easier to book, an all-inclusive price or warmer welcome.

A strong brand image also makes a difference, especially if physical characteristics are almost indistinguishable. Airlines are a good example of this. They use the same type of aircraft to fly the same routes, often at quite similar prices, with the same basic services. The difference comes in the way they all develop different brands and identities, investing vast sums of money to develop customer loyalty, brand recognition and appeal.

By focusing on niche markets

A business that targets different customers from its competitors will succeed more easily, but it is essential that it really does understand its customers. Some of the most successful companies have become highly profitable simply because they target just one sector of the population and really understand their customers so they can provide them with exactly what they need. A good example of this is the tour operator Saga, which offers holidays only for people over 50.

It can seem a little scary to take the decision to focus on a particular niche market, because it is always tempting to try to offer 'something for everyone'. However, as long as the business does understand its target market, it will be more successful with a niche approach than a general, broad-brush one.

A focused approach means concentrating on particular markets, understanding their needs completely, and therefore developing products and promotions which are completely appropriate for those markets. This approach requires an excellent knowledge of the chosen markets, and insight to direct all marketing efforts precisely. It is equally important to anticipate changes in the market place as well as demands for new products and services.

To develop your competitive edge, ask yourself:

■ What makes your product/service better or different from your competitors'?

■ What are the benefits (not features) of it to your customers?

■ How are you offering exactly what your customers need?

■ Why should anyone buy your product/service rather than your competitors'?

Remember that the majority of tourism products are made up of many different elements. The 'product' is not just one thing, but a total experience which includes:

▓ physical characteristics;

▓ greeting and welcome;

▓ how people are treated during the 'experience', whether it is a flight, week's tour, overnight stay, visit to an attraction, or football match;

▓ how easy the location/venue is to find and how accessible it is;

▓ other feelings such as those of security or comfort and relaxation;

▓ how closely the experience matches the promises of promotional material.

Sometimes judgements are made on seemingly peripheral elements such as the cleanliness of the toilets!

DEFINE YOUR UNIQUE SELLING POINT

It is said that around 85 per cent of all decisions, whether personal or business, are made by emotion rather than logic. It is often our 'gut reaction' which convinces us to do something, even in business situations.

These are some questions you might ask yourself about your product to help you develop a 'Unique Selling Point':

▓ What emotions will customers feel when they hear or read about your product or service?

▓ Will it save your customers money, make them money, or make them look as if they have money?

▓ Will it save them time in some way, or help them enjoy their time more?

▓ Does it offer them relaxation or relief from stress? Can it make them happy? Can it improve health?

▓ Could your product or service make your customers proud or help them to achieve something?

▓ Will it make them look or feel younger? Does it involve romance?

▓ Will it make them feel as if they 'belong' and give them security, either by fitting in or becoming part of an exclusive group?

Consider the answers to these questions. Is there just one element that you can focus on, that marks you out from your competition? This will be your Unique Selling Point or USP.

BE AWARE OF MARKET TRENDS

Your business is not run in isolation from the rest of the world so there are always other issues that you will need to take into consideration in your marketing plan. Keeping an eye on trends and changes in the wider world can help you develop interesting new ideas and business opportunities. You should be aware of general trends such as:

▓ the state of the economy and that of any of your overseas markets;

▓ markets and market segments which are growing or declining;

▓ changes in leisure and holiday-taking habits, such as the increased trend towards independent travel, increase in the number of short-break takers or increased demand for special interest holidays;

▓ technological developments, such as those outlined in chapter 1.

SELECT YOUR PROMOTIONAL TOOLS

The promotional tools you use will essentially be determined by your target markets and marketing budget. A blanket approach will not be as successful as one that pays careful consideration to each market segment and its needs.

Here are some of the factors that should influence your choice of promotional tools.

Target markets

What promotional methods are your customers used to? Is it better to use the ones that they accept and which experience proves they react to, or perhaps make an impact by trying something different?

Consider also whether you need to promote to end users or to intermediaries who can influence end users. These two groups will be stimulated by different kinds of messages.

Your product

How complex is your product or service? Some need more explanation than others. For example, services that need more detailed explanation are best promoted either using face-to-face selling, the Internet or print material.

Competition

Keep an eye on your competition because sometimes you will need to react according to their promotional activities.

Product awareness

New products that are just being launched generally need more promotion than established ones, but older products that are perhaps becoming stale will also need an extra push from time to time. If you are to choose the most appropriate promotional tools, you need to be aware of how much your potential customers know about you and how much information they need.

Stages in buying

Most customers move through fives stages when they decide to buy anything. Each of these stages needs different types of promotional material and messages (Table 6.1).

Table 6.1 *Matching messages to buying stages*

Buying Stage	Message
Unawareness At this stage your potential customers have never heard of you and don't know what you have to offer or whether it would be good for them. You also don't know these potential customers yet so you can't target them directly.	General awareness raising and focusing on persuasion rather than information
Awareness Potential customers have heard of you but haven't yet shown any interest in buying from you.	Still general, persuasive messages but information becoming more detailed
Understanding A very important stage where your potential customers have started to think about what you offer and show interest in it. They are now asking what's in it for me? How can I really benefit? You probably have a much clearer idea now who these potential customers are and what makes them tick.	Information much more detailed to show how your potential customers can benefit, anticipating and answering any questions they might have

Table 6.1 (continued)

Buying Stage	Message
Conviction	
Your customers fully understand what you have to offer and have seen how they could benefit. They have become convinced that your product is for them. You also now know much more about them. You may even know their names and addresses because they have made a further request for information. At this stage, it's still possible to lose customers through inertia (many want to buy something but never quite get round to doing anything about it) and not gently pushing them into purchase action or because you don't provide appropriate information to overcome any concerns.	Very detailed information although it still needs to be persuasive. Key messages now aim to push the customer into action, providing information on different ways of booking or buying from you and overcoming any final concerns they may have
Purchase	
You've overcome all the barriers and you know quite a lot about your customers because they've now made the transition from wanting to buy from you, to actually buying. The challenge isn't over – you want these customers to keep buying from you and telling other people how good you are.	You now need to focus on satisfying your customers and making sure they're happy with you, in order to persuade them to buy from you again. You also want to find ways to encourage them to recommend you to others.

MARKETING ACTION PLAN

Use the following checklist to make sure you have thought about all aspects of your marketing plan.

Current situation

■ What is the product or experience you are offering?
■ What are the key benefits?
■ Who are your current customers?
■ What general trends might affect your business, negatively or positively?

Conducting a SWOT analysis

Strengths

■ Your location – is it easily accessible, convenient, obvious and simple to find?
■ Staff – are they professional and friendly, or do they have some special skills such as languages which make you superior to your competitors?
■ Service – do you offer a good level of service or really broad range of services?
■ Marketing – do you have a high profile, strongly established market, or use innovative marketing methods?

Weaknesses

■ Your location – perhaps it is the reverse of the above?
■ Reputation and image – could it be better?
■ Staff – do they need more training or do you have staff shortages?
■ Services – could they improved in some way?
■ Internal problems – such as bad organization or reactive instead of proactive management.

Opportunities

■ Trends or fashions.
■ Changes in population.
■ Developments such as new technology.

Threats

■ Competition – what are your competitors up to? Perhaps there are some new developments which might affect your business?
■ Economic effects – such as a recession, high inflation or unemployment.
■ Developments – changes listed as opportunities may also be threats.

Conclusions from the SWOT analysis

▓ How can you maximize those strengths and opportunities?
▓ What can you do to minimize those weaknesses and threats?

Competitor analysis

▓ Who are your competitors?
▓ What do they offer?
▓ What are their prices – how do yours compare?
▓ What are their markets?
▓ How do they promote themselves?
▓ What are the relative advantages and disadvantages of their product compared with yours?
▓ How can you learn from them?
▓ Are there any opportunities you could exploit which they are missing?

Competitive advantage

▓ How are you going to compete?
▓ What is your Unique Selling Point?

Target markets

▓ Which will be your target markets?
▓ What more do you need to know about them and their needs?

Promotional tools

▓ What promotional tools will you use and how?
  – Brochure and print material?
  – Advertising?
  – PR activities?
  – Direct mail?
  – The Internet?
  – Sales activities?

Marketing objectives and monitoring

▓ What objectives do you want your marketing plan to achieve?
▓ How will you know if it has been successful?
▓ What timescale and deadlines have you set?
▓ What methods will you use to monitor the effects of your marketing activities?
▓ When will you do that?
▓ When will you review your marketing plan and develop a new one?

7

WEB SITES WITH IMPACT

When we first started to use the Internet, it was almost enough to simply have a site. Anyone who did was ahead of the game and even reaped some of the benefits of being 'first to market'.

Now it is not enough just to upload the pictures and words from your brochure. You need to think far more about the contents and structure of your site, how people will find it and what it is supposed to do. A couple of pages with photos of your visitor attraction might tell potential visitors that it is a wonderful place, but could equally fail to commit them to an actual visit. More experienced Webmasters are able to use their Web site to sell tickets and merchandise to make a profit out of visitors they have not yet met.

Web sites tend to evolve through four stages: they move from being purely informational to become interactive, then transactional and finally to build customer relationships, which encourage referrals and repeat visits.

1 The first stage is to simply offer information, usually in a not too dissimilar format to the brochures produced by most tourism and leisure organizations.
2 The second stage takes advantage of one of the great benefits of the Internet: it is interactive and enables users to see only the information they are interested in. Instead of scrolling through pages of general information and having to read about educational visits in order to see whether the

tea shop is likely to be open on a Wednesday afternoon, users can select only the subjects they are interested in.

3   The third stage is the one that webmasters should at least aspire to. When Web sites become transactional and it is possible to make bookings or buy from them, they start to pay for themselves and make it far more likely that a potential visitor or guest will not just look at your venue but make a commitment to coming to experience it for themselves.

4   In an ideal world, it would then be possible to move on to the next stage which involves developing a profitable and ongoing relationship with the user. This means that they not only return to your site again and again, but continue to contribute to your revenue stream, either directly or indirectly (by telling their friends about you). Of course, this is only an ideal situation and many Web sites do not even manage to convey information effectively.

This chapter aims to help you develop a site which is easy to use and has good content, with the kind of information and services that users are looking for. There are plenty of books, magazines and even free online tutorials dealing with how to build a Web site so this chapter does not duplicate information about the technical aspects of building a site.

PLANNING YOUR SITE

You can avoid making some expensive mistakes by planning the contents and development of your site before handing over to a technical consultant or designer. Try to answer some of the questions below before you begin.

Consider first of all exactly who your customers are and what they are looking for when they use your Web site. You need to draw up a comprehensive customer profile and to segment your markets just as you would when developing any other marketing activity. Chapter 2 looks at who is online and how they are using the Internet.

You will need to list your target markets, considering aspects such as:

▓ Are they existing or potential customers? What do they already know about you and what will they need to know in order to buy from you or be interested in your services?

▓ What are their ages and life-stages?

▓ What are their interests?

▓ Where are they from?

▓ Are they consumers, or 'influencers' like members of the travel trade?

▓ What are their motivations? Why would they buy from you or make a booking with you?

Next, make a list of all the different types of information your target customers are likely to be looking for, and the kind of functions your Web site will need to fulfil. You need to avoid hiding the most important information in the innermost pages of the Web site, just as you should make straightforward information like your address and contact details easy to find.

Draw a diagram showing the information customers will look for, when and in what order, so that you can create a site plan, similar to a tree diagram or organizational chart. Indicate how everything will link together and the sequence of material.

It is better to do this before you approach a designer. You should be in a better position than a designer, no matter how experienced, to know what your customers are looking for and how they will want to find that information. You will probably save money if you develop your own site plan instead of subcontracting it.

Before you start work on your site, take a careful look at your competitors' Web sites. Are there any lessons you can learn from them? Make a list of their best and worst features.

Consider whether you can develop or re-develop your Web site in phases. That way you can learn as you go and ensure that each phase is as good as possible before you start to develop the next. You will also be able to take advantage of feedback from customers and others.

Make sure you have clarified who will have control of your site. In its initial stages you will probably need the support of a technical team, which might include the IT department of your company. But make sure their input is restricted to technical support and ensuring the site functions properly, not controlling its longer-term development and content. A Web site should be the responsibility of marketers as an additional channel of communication with your customers, not a technical tool.

BUDGETING FOR YOUR SITE

You can build a Web site for anything upwards of around £2,000, but it could equally cost nearer £50,000–£100,000 if you want to develop a complex database-driven site that will enable you to take bookings online. With such a vast range of options, it would be simpler to set a budget and find a way of working within it, either by learning to develop the site yourself or by shopping around for the right designer and technical support.

Whatever budget you allocate, bear in mind that there will be not only a one-off set-up cost, but also ongoing development costs. These will include the cost of maintaining your domain name and the space where your site is hosted, as well as improvements to the site.

If you decide that you need to keep costs to a minimum, you can build your own site using established and relatively easy-to-use software such as Microsoft Frontpage or Macromedia's Dreamweaver. These packages do not require you to learn HTML (the code behind most Web sites) or have any real programming skills.

However, unless you are particularly skilled in that area, it would be worthwhile getting a designer to devise a suitable layout for your home page so you present a professional image. You can then follow the suggested layout for subsequent pages and focus your attention on ensuring that you have appropriate content for the site.

REGISTERING A DOMAIN NAME

A domain name is a text name which is used as a convenient way to find sites on the Internet and to provide an easy-to-remember address. Registering a domain name on the Internet is similar to registering a company name at Companies House. Once registered (and as long as you continue to own the name), the name is yours and cannot be used by anyone else.

Different countries have different rules about the names you can register. In some countries the rules are very complex, whereas in others it is something of a 'free for all'. You can check if the name you would like to use has already been registered and find out more about the rules affecting registration in different countries by going to a Web site operated by a domain-name-registration company like www.netbenefit.co.uk. Now that some of the search engines are becoming so vast, some of them only include domain names relevant to specific country sites. This means that only co.uk sites might be listed on a British version of a search engine.

Domain names have to be cleared by the relevant country registry (NOMINET in the UK) and then a certificate of registration is issued. The suffix after the name, such as .com or .co.uk, indicates the type of organization and the country where it was registered. .com is the most popular name for a commercial organization and is seen as being international. The other domain names that have already been established are:

■ commercial companies – co.uk;

■ non-commercial organizations – org.uk;

■ limited companies – .ltd.uk;

■ Public Limited Companies – .plc.uk;

■ academic institutions – ac.uk;

■ government organizations including boroughs and councils – gov.uk.

In addition to the much sought-after domain names of .com and co.uk, the Internet Corporation for Assigned Names and Numbers (ICANN) has now introduced new domain names:

■ businesses – .biz;

■ co-operatives – .coop;

▨ general information – .info;

▨ museums – .museum;

▨ individuals – .name;

▨ professionals such as lawyers – .pro.

These new names were introduced to increase the range of domain names available, improve navigation on the Internet and minimize risks posed by 'cybersquatters' who register names that are not relevant to them in the hope of being able to sell them at a profit later.

You can register as many relevant names as you want to ensure that users find your site. A number of organizations that originally registered cumbersome and difficult names are now registering more appropriate ones 'pointing' at the same site. You might also want to register names in different countries so that you can have 'virtual offices'. When registering a name you should ensure that it does not infringe the rights of any other organizations.

UK names can be anything from 3 to 64 characters long and can include numbers (so you could have a domain name that is an easy-to-remember telephone number) but no punctuation except for hyphens, which are normally seen as a space.

Short names are easier to remember and there is less danger that users will make a mistake when typing the name and risk not finding you. If your name is one that is often spelt incorrectly, it may be worth registering the incorrect version as well as the correct one.

Domain names are case insensitive but are usually given as lower case. Sometimes, however, it is a good idea to write the domain name with some capitals in it to make it easier to read and remember – for example, www.VisitBritain.com.

Make sure your name is easy to remember and relates to your organization or what you do. If the name you want is already registered you might need to think laterally and creatively about another relevant name. For example, a restaurant with a common name that has already been registered might choose to register something like www.foodlovers.co.uk instead.

If you ask someone else such as a Web site designer to register the domain name on your behalf, make sure that the certificate of registration is in your name and not theirs so that you actually own the site.

DESIGNING YOUR WEB SITE

It is interesting that almost as much is written about aspects of Web design that do not work as those that do. You might need to consider working with two different kinds of company or people. There seem to be few designers who are good at the technical aspects of building a Web site and few technicians who are also capable of producing designs that look good. This means it is often worthwhile working with a designer *and* a developer.

Even if you are working to a limited budget, be wary of choosing the cheapest designers. They may be good and cheap but could be charging a lower fee because they want to get a chance to learn about Web site design – at your expense. Whoever you work with, ensure that they do have some Web site design experience, even if they have not worked directly on a project like yours. They do not necessarily need to have had experience of working on tourism or hospitality-related projects, but they will need to understand your business and what your customers are looking for.

Be careful too of choosing designers who might want to impose their ideas and use the latest animation tools simply because they have learnt them and want to put them into action. You need to be confident that any designers you choose will follow your brief and create a site suitable for your target audience, not as a shop-front for their more advanced design skills.

Be very clear about exactly what services your Web site designers are going to undertake. These are some of the issues you will need to think about:

▓ Will they simply design the site or build it as well?

▓ Will they upload it and continue to work on your behalf until the site is 'live' and free of any initial glitches?

■ Will they show you how to update the site or will you be forever beholden to them for even the smallest change?

■ Will they register the site with the search engines or will you need to do that?

■ When will they hand over the finished site and all the associated files to you?

■ Who will own the copyright of the site?

■ What level of after-sales care and support can you expect?

SAMPLE WEB SITE DESIGN BRIEF

Your Web site design brief will need to be as comprehensive and detailed as possible, including the maximum amount of information about your aims and objectives. It should include a range of points.

Background

Details about your company such as when it was established, what its aims are, what it does, why you need a Web site and what you want it to achieve.

Nature and scope of the project

This section should describe the identity of the site and what you expect the designer to do. It should contain a summary of what your site will include. For example, the name of the site, the type of content it will have, likely links and any other relevant information.

Design issues

A description of the target audience for the site will be useful here, explaining what sort of 'look' and personality the site will need to have.

Here are some sample angles that you might want to include in this section:

■ Navigating the Web site must be as intuitive as is practical.

■ The site should feel uncluttered, despite the wealth of information it will ultimately contain. Users must feel positively about it. They shouldn't feel confused, or as if they are missing more information than they are accessing. It must also be remembered that many users will not be completely familiar with using the Web.

■ For the most part, design must be led by content.

■ All content must download as quickly as possible. The site may require a large number of images but the pages must be made to load as quickly as possible. The site should be made as interactive and engaging as possible by innovative use of ordinary effects (links, changing images, roll-overs etc) rather than overloading the site with lots of Flash or Shockwave and the like. The message of the site should be clear at all times.

■ Users should be encouraged to make frequent repeat visits to the site. The site must feel active.

■ Users should be encouraged to give feedback and to be able to send information back to the Webmaster, for example through use of forms.

Technical constraints

You should describe the level of your technical knowledge. For example, do you have any knowledge of HTML? Are there any particular software packages which you would like the designers to use?

You might ask the designers to use software such as Microsoft Frontpage or Macromedia Dreamweaver and then ensure you receive training in these so that you can update and maintain the site. Another suggestion might be to ask the designer to create some of the site as easy to update and upload templates and then show you how to make changes.

Explain which Internet Service Provider is hosting your site and whether it is on a Unix or NT server. If you have not yet registered your site or decided which provider to use, ask for advice from the Web site developer.

It is useful to give an indication of what kind of technical capabilities your target audience are likely to have. This would involve knowing whether the majority of customers will view the site using Internet Explorer or Netscape Navigator, and which issue, whether they are likely to have large or small monitor screens, and so on. However, it is usually difficult to be certain of this information, although you are likely to know whether your target audience would welcome or reject additional features such as animations that need 'plug-ins' to view them.

Intellectual property agreements

Ensure that all copyright, design rights and trademark ownership for unrestricted and exclusive use will be transferred to you upon completion of the site development and payment of the appropriate design and development fees.

Timescale

You will need to set a timescale with deadlines for the different stages of development of the site. These are likely to include:

▦ Design: when do you need design ideas developed as roughs, and when should they be worked into the agreed finished solution, ready for transfer to the Web?

▦ Site development: when will the site plan be created? With what input from you? When will the designer present flat visuals of sample content and the home page (either hard or electronic copy)? What are the deadlines for converting site content (presumably to be provided by you)?

▦ When will the site be built and when will it be tested? When will it formally go 'live'?

▩ What is the 'hand-over' date, when the site and associated files will be handed over to you?

DESIGN AND CONTENT PITFALLS TO AVOID

The following is a brief round-up of things that irritate users and pitfalls to avoid.

Sites that are hard to navigate

Some sites are difficult to navigate because they do not follow design conventions such as a left-hand menu bar. One of the reasons mooted for the demise of the ill-fated online clothes retailer boo.com is that the site was too difficult to use, with key links like 'buy it' hidden behind quirky design features.

Some sites suffer from information overload. They are so cluttered that users either cannot find what they are looking for or have a sense that each time they follow a link from the home page they are missing something potentially more useful, or that they will not find their way back again.

Slow loading

Consumer research indicates that most users do not want to wait much longer than 10 seconds for a site to load. Sites with heavy graphics and images are unlikely to load that quickly so users simply move away.

Out-of-date sites

Despite the ease of updating Web sites, too many sites contain out-of-date information.

Bad targeting

Apparently in over 60 per cent of cases, users do not get past the home page because they have no idea what the site is supposed to do or are disappointed in the information available. Too many home pages make ambitious promises that are not fulfilled by the actual content.

Contact details

It is often surprisingly difficult either to make bookings or to find out who is behind the development and operation of some Web sites. Contact details are frequently hidden several layers deep on pages that do not have a direct link from the home page.

Tedious registration process

When you ask users to register before being able to use the site, you deter them from staying. Surveys have found that almost half of users leave sites when asked to register before they are allowed to access the site or obtain even the most basic information. This is not the same as asking users to register details in order to customize the site or to receive special or additional information. An earlier Toyota Web site had a log-in/registration request on its home page that was not actually compulsory but appeared to be. When it was removed, the number of hits is said to have increased by 1,500 per day.

Not clear what to do

Because they use unusual design or do not carry sufficient instructions, some sites are difficult to use. It may not be clear how to navigate the site, what information is where and which aspects of the text are links to other parts of the site.

GENERAL DESIGN TIPS

■ Ensure that the site is easy to read. Although Webmasters naturally want to make their site stand out from the rest, the best colour scheme to use is black or very dark text on a white or light background. Fonts need to be legible and of a decent size. Too many moving or flashing objects on the page detract from the clarity of text.

■ Do not assume a high level of knowledge on the part of the user. With so many new users getting online every day, many people are still only just getting to grips with how the Internet works and ways to navigate sites.

Users will arrive at your site with different levels of skills and experience. You will need to anticipate and cater for these. For example, if you provide some information as a 'pdf' file you will need to explain what this is and that the user needs Adobe Acrobat Reader to access it. By explaining how to download the Reader and providing a direct link to do so, you will encourage more people to access your information. If you take this one step further and stress how easy it is to download the Reader and how it can then be used for many other purposes, you will encourage even more users.

■ Do not be too clever. Flash animations might look interesting but not everyone has the necessary software to view them. Although Flash can add life to creative sites, it is more likely to get in the way of speed on more commercial sites. Assume a lower rather than higher level of technical knowledge. Since many users will not have installed Flash or may have disabled the ability to see Flash animations, you might need to offer a text-only alternative.

■ It is useful to stick with conventional design, which means mirroring the majority of sites that use a left-hand menu for navigation purposes. Only underline words when they are actually links, or make the links within your site very clear.

■ Be specific in the instructions you give to help users navigate your site, with straightforward prompts such as 'click here'. Make it quite clear where the links are within your site; do not hide too many of them behind icons and other buttons.

■ Make sure the pages of your Web site are easy to print as many users prefer to print pages of text and read them offline later. If for any reason it is not easy to print them, make sure you give as many instructions as necessary.

▓ Images and photographs can bring your Web site to life. Consumers do expect to see pictures of accommodation, holiday destinations and so on, to whet their appetite and give them a sense of security. However, images will slow down the loading of your site. Make sure that any illustrations have been 'optimized', to make them quicker to load.

It is a good idea to give users a choice of whether they want to see lots of photographs or not. You can do this by providing a link to a 'photo gallery' rather than displaying photos on every page, and also by providing small-size or 'thumb-nail' images that can be enlarged by clicking on them.

▓ Research suggests that only about 10 per cent of users scroll beyond the information immediately seen on their screen. This has several implications. If your site requires the user to read a lot of text, make sure you layer the information, putting the most important first.

Suggest to readers that they print off the page. Some users will want to scroll down the page to read all the text, but you should break this up by using keywords and 'anchor points' (link words that, when clicked on, will take the user to another part of the page). Make sure you do not put important or navigational information at the bottom of the page.

▓ Your home page needs to make a strong impact. Use a friendly, bright and very clear style and make the purpose of the site immediately obvious. If it is possible to make online bookings on your site, say so and provide a direct link to that area. If it is not you must also say so and provide a direct and obvious link to your contact details.

▓ Some users will have reached your site by clicking on a link from another site. This may mean that they arrive in the middle of your site, instead of the home page. Make it clear what site each page belongs to and provide a menu on every page so users can see what other information is available. It should always be easy to return to the home page.

CONSIDERING THE PERSONALITY OF YOUR WEB SITE

The information in your Web site is at least as important as the design and layout of the site. You will need to decide what kind of site you want and what kind of 'mood' you aim to convey. Do you want to exude professionalism and/or friendliness? Do you want immediately to convey a strong sense of your own personality, reassuring potential guests that you are not running an impersonal branded service? The personality of your Web site can help you to develop your overall competitive advantage.

One hotelier I know runs a 2-star hotel in Bloomsbury surrounded by lots of other quite similar hotels. This particular hotel manager has a strong sense of humour and greets guests like old friends, but at the same time he is anxious to make sure his hotel is clean and a world away from some of the stereotypes of London budget hotels with uncertain hygiene standards. His Web site totally reflects his personality. Instead of just saying that the hotel is friendly and clean, it shows a photograph of him holding a mop, and plenty of other pictures showing staff holding mops or even cleaning the toilets. Every page within his home-made site conveys a sense of his personality and is written in such a friendly style the site is worth seeing even if you are not planning a trip to London (www.eurohotel.co.uk).

One of the advantages of Web sites is that they offer the same level of promotion to a small operator as to a large one. When you first enter a Web site it is not always obvious if there is a huge organization behind it or just one person. This can also be a disadvantage because some Web sites appear faceless and unfriendly. Make sure you give yours personality, even if you do not want it to be informal. Ensure there is a part of your site where users can find out about the people behind it.

WRITING COPY FOR WEB SITES

There are three key differences between writing copy for a Web site and for a brochure:

▪ You will need to write shorter, more concise copy for the Web site because users tend to scan information rather than scroll through long pages of text.

▪ You will probably need to work harder online to create consumer confidence in what you offer, partly because it is a new medium and less tangible than other promotional tools.

▪ You will need to break up and layer the information for your Web site according to different consumer needs, taking advantage of the interactivity of the Internet to present content in the order that the user wants. A series of short passages of information, just a few clicks away from each other, is the most appropriate way to present content on the Internet.

If you know your customers well, you should have a good idea of the language they use and how much persuading they will need. Do not overdo this and 'hype' your service if you do not think it is appropriate for your target market. Read through what you have written and ask yourself whether you would believe it. If you think it sounds too good to be true, then you will either need to tone it down or justify the assertions you are making.

If you are trying to make people buy, as well as informing them, try to follow the basic process outlined below.

Step 1: make an offer, or a promise or tell your reader what you can do for them

This should be enticing information that 'hooks' them in as readers. Make sure it is a realistic promise or synopsis of what you or your site can do.

Step 2: give a little more information about what you can do and the services you offer

If your hook was good, readers will be interested and want to know more about what you offer, so this is a good place to offer supplementary information, but don't give too much – leave them wanting to know more.

Step 3: offer some reassurance

It is a sad fact that most of the time when we are made an offer or promise, we are initially interested and then we think, 'How can that be? It's too good to be true. What's the catch?' At this point you need to be aware that your customers may have become cynical and are in need of some reassurance. Even if they are not already thinking it, they will appreciate the reassurance. Ways of reassuring your customers include:

■ explaining why you are making the offer – 'off-peak reductions' and so on;

■ money back guarantees or other guarantees of satisfaction;

■ information about previous satisfied customers. This needs to be credible and if possible, backed up with factual information. For example, 'xx per cent of our customers are repeat customers or referred to us by other satisfied customers'.

Step 4: offer more information

Your potential customers will hopefully now be feeling more reassured and therefore open to receiving more information, so you should give it to them. This is the time to clarify all the details of what you are offering and suggest other sources of information.

Step 5: push your customer into action

Even if your customers are now completely convinced, they will probably need pushing into action in order to buy from you or make a booking. This means that you might offer a discount or make an added-value offer. Giving a deadline for response is a good idea; around two weeks usually works quite well. Or you might just need to make sure your telephone number for bookings is large and clear with a call to action like 'call us now'.

DEVELOPING YOUR HOME OR INTRODUCTION PAGE

This is the first page that users of your Web site will see. They will take a quick glance at it and almost instantly decide whether to stay on the site. If it takes ages to load or looks particularly uninviting you will lose them before the site has even fully loaded. Users will scan the content and decide what to do next.

If it appears to contain enough relevant information they will click on a link and move into the main body of the site. If it looks too complicated or seems to have too much information to deal with there and then, they will either move away or perhaps print off the information or bookmark the site to revisit later. And then probably forget about it.

This means that you need to make the same sort of impact on your home page as you would try to do on the front page of your brochure. However, there are some important differences. You probably use a big image on the front page of your brochure, which you should avoid doing on your Web site because it will take too long to load. Also, you rely on people seeing the rest of the brochure for the main part of information and they probably turn over at least one page to look for it. On the Web, you have to make it clear what your site does, straight away.

Use your home page to give a very brief introduction of what you do and what your site offers. Provide strong clear links to all the information you think users need and put the most important first. Do not think you can use supermarket techniques and get shoppers to walk through the whole shop to look for the milk and bread. You cannot entice users to read more information by burying the key facts deep in your site – they will not even enter it.

Grab attention

You need to grab attention on every page but particularly on your home page, and to cater for the vast majority of users who will only scan your pages, without reading every word.

Make it easy for people to scan effectively. If you highlight keywords that jump out at readers, their eyes will automatically be 'locked in' to them and read the text around the key word.

Decide what are the most important words your target markets are likely to be looking for. You need to do this in order to use the right keywords for search engines (see chapter 8 for a more detailed explanation), but also to make each page of your Web site interesting. For example, if you run a visitor attraction aimed at families, words like 'children', 'parents' and 'fun' will jump out at your visitors.

You probably need a couple of headings on each page to break up the text and grab the users' attention.

Because the home page is usually just an overview of the whole site, it is easy to think you can write it very quickly. In fact, this is the one page that you should spend some time on, because if you lose a visitor here, you have basically lost them for ever.

Make sure that there are plenty of points in your home page where you encourage users to click to the next page. To encourage users to read more and to click through for more information, you will need to keep your paragraphs short and pages compact without long, dense wads of text. You should also use various navigation tools to encourage click-throughs. These might include: a button with an arrow on it; a button that says 'next page'; the words 'click here to. . .'

It is a good idea to include links within sentences (for example, 'click here to find out how to benefit'). Incomplete sentences also work well to entice the reader to find out more.

GENERAL COPYWRITING TIPS

Here are some tips to help you present information that users will want to read:

▤ You will be able to write more persuasive and direct copy if you picture one typical reader in your mind. This will help you write as if you were speaking to one person. What sort of words and ideas will individuals react to? You will grab your readers' attention by addressing them directly, using words like 'you'. YOU instantly grabs attention. Readers identify with it and instinctively assume it means them.

▤ Headlines are useful for attracting attention. Responses will be more positive if you:

– make a promise (one you can fulfil)

– offer the solution to a problem

– describe a good strong benefit.

▤ Link your headline to the first sentence of the main text so readers are enticed into reading on. It is worth starting with something newsworthy or different, a surprising fact rather than a standard introduction.

▤ Use specifics, not generalizations; '*beautiful settings, great food, friendly service*' works better than '*something for everyone*'.

▤ Short everyday words, short sentences and short paragraphs are easier to read. Short sentences have most impact.

▤ Break up your text and keep it short. Use plenty of headings to make your pages easy to read by scanning. Do not use paragraphs that are longer than two or three sentences of no more than about 12 words. You can also put some keywords in bold to make them stand out. Capital letters are harder to read. Text should only be underlined if it is a link.

▤ Lists and bullet points are easier to read than blocks of text. One reason for this is because they need white space around them, which draws the eye in to the text.

▤ Avoid using jargon, and if you need to use it, make sure you define it.

▤ Try not to write stilted English as if it was part of a school essay. To check if your copy sounds stilted, read what you have written aloud and see if it makes you cringe!

■ Remember that people like anecdotes and mini-stories; this is often a good way of convincing your users.

■ Make sure your font size is consistent and do not use too many different-sized fonts; this gives a jumbled look and is difficult to read.

IMPROVING YOUR SITE

However good your Web site is, it will never be truly finished. Just as you continue to introduce new services, recruit new staff, refurbish and find new ways of promoting your services, you will now also have to keep updating and improving your Web site so that it remains fresh-looking and ahead of the competition. Remember that for many potential visitors, your brochure and Web site are the only tangible evidence of what you offer, so they need to reflect the best of your services.

If you pride yourself on your customer service, you will want to reflect this on your Web site. Simply saying, 'we offer excellent customer service' will not impress; you will need to find ways of building credibility and demonstrating just how you offer great service. One way of doing this is by offering additional information on your Web site.

Web sites that encourage users to feel most positive about the companies behind them usually have three levels of content:

1 Core information about the company's product or services. For example, a hotel would include details about rooms and other facilities, prices and perhaps an online booking facility.
2 Enhanced information that sets the product or service in context or helps the user feel more informed, even if this content is slightly peripheral to the actual product or service being promoted. A hotel might include a currency converter, weather forecast or links to more information about the location of the hotel.
3 Inspirational or persuasive information that encourages the user to imagine why they might want to buy that product and find reasons for doing so. A hotel's Web site might have plenty of information about things to do in the area, local history and recommendations for local pubs or attractions.

Here are some of the optional extras you might consider putting on your Web site. You can either develop the information yourself or link to other sites that offer it. If you are worried about losing site visitors to other sites when you provide links, you can make the linked site open up as a mini browser-window so users do not actually move away from your site.

Some Web sites have **different entry points for different users**, depending on the user. Take a look at www.visitbritain.com and you will see that it asks where you are coming from so you can be taken to the most relevant site, with tailor-made 'gateway' sites for different geographic markets.

Taking this approach means you can link with other relevant companies and benefit from cross-referrals. For example, if you are based in Britain and have customers coming from Germany, it might be an idea to link with one of the Anglophile bookstores based somewhere like Frankfurt, or with an airline flying to and from Germany.

Your basic Web site might not change, but there could be a few additional pages of relevant and tailored content that certain users see before being taken to the main site.

If you deal with people from all over the world, do you need to offer **translated versions** of your Web site? You can either get your site professionally translated or link to one of the translation sites that automate the process. Their version will never be as good as one translated by a mother-tongue professional but will at least show you are trying to be helpful. You might also need to think about registering different domain names in different countries.

The Hyatt hotel chain found that travellers were much more likely to seek information and book via the Internet if the content of Web sites was translated into their own language. They conducted two tests. A Chinese site was developed for the Grand Hyatt in Taipei and got 13 times the traffic of the English version. Sites in German for their German hotels also got four times the traffic of the English versions.

Visitors to your site will appreciate being given **information about complementary services**. Make your site more of a 'one-stop info shop' by linking to other relevant suppliers and providing more comprehensive information. Try to use links that competing companies might not have thought of. For example, you could link to www.booktailor.com who provide tailor-made guidebooks according to the readers' preferences, rather than to a more mainstream company.

A **currency converter** is a useful add-on to any Web site that attracts users from overseas. **Weather reports and forecasts** are popular, but you could go one step further by offering suggestions for activities in your area or related to your company that are suitable for different types of weather: 'great places to eat ice-cream', '10 ways to enjoy sheltering from the rain'.

www.cheapflights.co.uk is an example of a site that offers a great range of links. If you choose a destination, you will find links to relevant airlines and travel agencies as well as guide-book publishers, weather forecasts, currency converters, accommodation booking agencies and others.

Providing travel directions and maps can be problematic due to map licensing restrictions. You can bypass those difficulties by linking to sites that offer **maps and traffic reports**. Details of some of these are included in chapter 12.

Whether you run a hotel, visitor attraction or other leisure company, visitors to your site are likely to appreciate information about your local area. Rather than just including official sites like those given by tourist boards, consider including information from smaller organizations like local history societies.

A **media room** containing press releases and archived newsletters is invaluable. It is a particularly useful way to handle out-of-hours media enquiries and good to refer journalists to when they need extra information in a hurry.

Competitions and special offers will keep your site fresh and interesting, and the novelty factor will keep users coming back to see what's new. They also offer another opportunity to gather data about participants (but always make sure you ask their permission to use any information gathered in this way).

One way of encouraging users to keep returning to your site is to ensure that you have fresh and stimulating content. One way of doing this it to build an **online community**. This is not relevant to every organization, but if you can do it successfully it should increase loyalty and provide a wider range of information, without too much input from you.

BUILDING AN ONLINE COMMUNITY

Most businesses appreciate the need to strengthen and maintain relationships with their customers and stakeholders. They need to build new markets by initiating dialogues and building confidence, even if this might not immediately reap financial rewards. Building an online community is effectively just another way of developing customer relationships, often at a fraction of the cost of the same type of activity offline.

There are several benefits to building an online community.

▓ Surveys by Forrester Research in 2000 found that people who participate in online communities tend to be committed and educated Internet users who are 37 per cent more likely to purchase online than non-community users. They also found that the type of products most favoured by community users were those associated with fun and 'the feel-good factor', so this approach is ideally suited to businesses in the tourism and hospitality industry. As an example, British Airways has a 'travel space' within its site that enables customers to put up their travel photographs and comments, and to chat with other members of the community.

▓ Another important advantage of building a community is that participants effectively keep Web sites fresh by contributing new and changing content for the site. They also keep returning to the site to see what's changed.

▓ Online communities can be useful for market research and to obtain feedback about new products and services. You can also use the community to initiate dialogues about products members might like to see in the future.

▓ Some communities have the added benefit of helping to cut down on customer-support costs by encouraging members to pose questions and ask other members for solutions to problems. This would also work well for tourism destinations, enabling members to ask others for recommendations about places to go and things to do.

Creating an online community – points to remember

■ Ensure that you offer content and information that is likely to stimulate debate and discussions.

■ Make sure there are plenty of reasons for people to participate.

■ Accept that the 'community' area of your site will not necessarily be sales-oriented for your organization, but should be more neutral. Sometimes this will mean accepting criticism and using it as positive feedback.

■ Consider using an FAQ (frequently asked question) section to avoid too much repetition in the community.

■ Ensure that you have systems in place to respond to any comments from the community that are directly related to your organization. You will need to ensure that you have a key member of staff whose responsibility is to sustain and feed the community with appropriate comments and to respond to feedback or suggestions.

■ If you start to build a community and find that it does not attract many visitors or postings, you will need to either stimulate more activity, promote the site or consider withdrawing that section from your site. A community area that is effectively a ghost town with only out-of-date information and responses will do more damage than good.

It can be hard to establish a vibrant community from scratch, so consider partnering with another established and relevant community, perhaps through sponsorship of particular activities.

Frequently asked questions (FAQs)

At some point, users of your site will have some questions about the service you offer. You should try to cover as much information as possible by not assuming too much prior knowledge. It is a good idea to get someone who does not know too much about what you do to read through the content of your site and see if they have any questions.

Once you have done this, even if you feel you have covered them somewhere in your site, make a list of the questions that your customers ask you most frequently – by phone, in person or by mail. It is a good idea to create a specific area of your Web site where you can list these questions and the appropriate responses. A popular approach that many sites are now embracing is to have a section called FAQs.

Feedback

Provide opportunities for your site users to give you feedback. This is a chance for them to interact with you, and for you to find out more about them and build a relationship. You might simply provide an e-mail link and invite feedback, or provide an online form or short questionnaire requesting comments and suggestions. If it is important for you to get users' feedback, it is a good idea to offer a small incentive to get them to fill out more information.

If a user takes the time to give you negative or positive feedback, make sure you respond to them. Try to avoid giving a standard response. If they are interested enough in your site to write to you, they are at least lukewarm about buying from you. Your response to their feedback, even if it is a negative comment, could make all the difference to your retaining them as a satisfied customer.

Updating your site

You will need to set a timetable for the ongoing development and updating of your site. How often will it be and when? Which areas of the site will be changed? Try to put some dates in your diary and, if you are brave enough, put the date of forthcoming changes on your Web site to make sure you stick to it! This also offers an ideal opportunity to encourage users to bookmark specific areas of the site because they will be updated – and another reason to e-mail users (assuming they have said they would like to receive e-mails from you) reminding them to revisit the site.

TESTING YOUR SITE

Once you have developed your site, you should test that it works, both technically and from a marketing perspective. Things to double-check are:

▨ Does it do what users expect it to do? Try using the site and check how easy it is to navigate. Keep asking yourself whether each page provides the information that users will need.

▨ Does the site function properly? Follow each of the external and internal links to make sure they are all live and relevant.

▨ Are you sure the site will still perform well if you suddenly get lots of users?

▨ Can the site be seen using different browsers? Do not assume every user will have the latest software and equipment.

▨ Is the site as secure as it needs to be? What have you done to reassure users and make them feel confident about using it?

Following this checklist will help you to make sure your site is easy to use and has a clear, attractive design.

▨ Is the navigation clear?

▨ Is the menu in an obvious place, easy to see, and shown on each page so it is possible to get to all areas of the site in the minimum number of 'clicks'?

▨ Does the site follow the same design throughout ?

▨ Is relevant information presented and requested at appropriate times? For example, users will not want to give their credit card details before they have had the chance to search for services they are interested in.

▮ Is there reassurance about credit card security?

▮ Is most information just three clicks away from the home page?

▮ Is the site really interactive?

▮ Does it make it possible for the users to obtain only the information they are interested in?

▮ Is the language clear?

▮ Does it avoid jargon that only some users will understand?

▮ Does it give clear, concise instructions to users?

▮ Is the text easy to read and understand?

▮ Is the content presented in 'bite-sized' chunks?

▮ If the site asks for data from the user, is it easy to input?

▮ Is it obvious exactly what is being asked?

▮ Does the site help to build your brand an overall identity?

▮ Is it instantly recognizable and in keeping with your other promotional activities?

▮ Is the design relevant to your target markets?

▮ Are principal concerns such as those about privacy addressed within the site?

▮ Is there an opportunity for users to give feedback?

▮ Would they be confident that they will receive a speedy response?

▮ Is the site updated at regular intervals?

▮ Does it state when it was last updated so users can gauge its accuracy?

Finally, have you established a programme for redevelopment and improvement? How will you respond to feedback from users? Have you identified specific members of staff to respond to e-mails and other enquiries and set ideal timescales for responses?

RESEARCH: THE ROLE OF THE INTERNET IN DESTINATION CHOICE

A market research study commissioned jointly by South East England Tourist Board and Southern Tourist Board and undertaken by MarketVoice Marketing Research Consultancy recently looked at the role of the Internet in destination choice. Four focus groups were held, two with participants aged 25+ and two with participants aged 45+. One of the criteria for selection of the participants was that they had used the Internet to search for holiday information in the past three months.

The research identified some of the main reasons for liking and disliking particular Web sites. These reasons are summarized below.

Main reasons for liking a site among the group of people 25+

- ease of use: easy to log on; quick, easy navigation;
- convenience: opportunity to pay online, goods delivered to the door;
- fun;
- source of information;
- access to other consumers;
- well-designed sites: clear and pictorial;
- good-value-for-money products.

Main reasons for liking a site among the group of people 45+

- ease of use: easy to log on, 'idiot proof', easy to understand, straightforward, quick, lots of links;
- convenience: available at any time; user can pay online when confident about security and company's reputation.

Main reasons for disliking a site among the group of people 25+

■ slow download: pictures which rarely download fully, pictures at the bottom of the page often missed, extraneous animation, having to wait, never arriving at a desired destination;

■ incomplete information: inability to deliver requirements, insufficient information;

■ unattractive home pages: home page too busy, poor design, poor use of colour, all text, difficulty in moving to next page;

■ users' aversion to giving out personal details such as e-mail address;

■ site that does not work easily.

Main reasons for disliking a site among the group of people 45+

■ slow download: pictures, animation;

■ requests to return to a site later;

■ poor layout: pictures out of focus, too much text;

■ lack of flexibility;

■ incomplete information: no prices, dates, product or service unavailable;

■ having to join or become a member;

■ advertising on sites;

■ no contact or customer service number;

■ information that cannot be viewed due to state of the art technology not being available on the average computer.

8

PROMOTING YOUR WEB SITE

Assuming that you have developed a site that incorporates the benefits of the Internet, you will want to promote it to the maximum number of users. If your Web site is part of an integrated marketing strategy, you will be able to inter-link all your promotional activities so that they can cross-fertilize each other.

This chapter deals with both online and offline promotion of your Web site, using traditional and new methods.

OFFLINE PROMOTIONAL ACTIVITIES

A memorable domain name

Promoting your Web site will be so much easier both online and offline if your domain name is memorable and easy to spell. Long names, or ones that do not relate well to your company and what it does, will be hard to remember and use.

If you have developed a Web site using a domain name that you think is not very easy to remember, you can register another one and 'point' it to your current site. You can also register different domain names to use in different kinds of promotion. For example, a leisure centre might have its own domain name based on the name of the centre but use a more interesting one for specific promotions. It could register and use a name like www.exhaust-the-kids.com for promotions during school holidays. See chapter 7 for more guidance on selecting domain names.

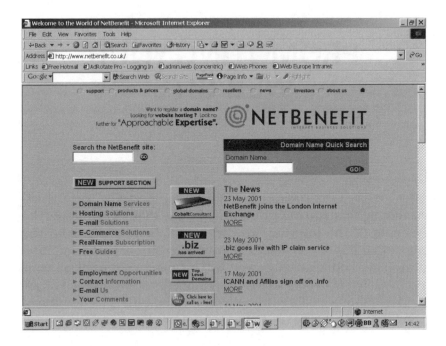

Figure 8.1 Registering a memorable **domain name** is a key way of generating visitors to your site

You might need to promote specific areas of your Web site from time to time so that potential customers access only relevant information. For example, a hotel chain's Web site probably includes a whole range of corporate information. If some (but not all) of the hotels want to promote some special offers, they may need to give a Web site address that takes users immediately to appropriate pages. If you want to do this, make sure you label each page and section of your Web site in a way that is likely to make sense to users, avoiding codes or abbreviations so that the sub-site address is as easy to remember as the main domain name.

Print material

Most tourism and leisure organizations are used to promoting themselves using print material. Leaflets and business cards will remain important and now need to take on the additional role of promoting your Web site.

Whenever you get any print material redesigned or printed, remember to add your Web site address. It should be displayed as visibly as possible on everything: your letterhead, business cards, brochures and so on.

Consider printing some materials specifically to promote your Web site. Postcards and bookmarks are relatively cheap to print and, providing they are attractive and lively, most people enjoy receiving and using them.

It is a good idea to devise a strap-line or one-line description of what your site does and the benefits it offers users. Remember to use this every time you quote your domain name on print material or in a press release.

You should also make sure that the identity of your site and your other print materials are closely aligned so that both are instantly recognizable as part of the same brand. Easyjet has been very successful in doing this and building a strong identity, basically by using a colour that is so bright and strong that few other organizations use it! Now, whenever we see their vibrant orange, whether it is on print material, the Web site or uniforms, we instantly think of Easyjet.

Word-of-mouth recommendation

Probably the most powerful form of promotion, word-of-mouth recommendations are more likely if your site has a clear and useful function and works well. If it is good, people will recommend your site to others, and most Internet users find this kind of referral far more credible than any other promotion. Sometimes users need prompting and reminding.

You can encourage them by adding a 'recommend this Web site to your friends' button on your Web site and making it easy for users to forward pages of the site to other people. www. thisislondon.com makes extensive use of this form of promotion, by displaying a 'forward this article to a friend' link at the bottom of the page.

You can also stimulate referrals at periodic intervals by changing and updating the content, perhaps by adding new elements like competitions.

Stimulating word-of-mouth recommendations (sometimes called 'word of mouse' on the Web!) is covered in more detail in chapter 10 under the heading of 'Viral marketing'.

Staff

Make sure that your staff know your Web site address and encourage people to look at it when appropriate. You will probably need to undertake some staff training to show them all how to use your Web site and enthuse them about the information it contains. This will help them talk about it more authoritatively instead of just giving out an odd-sounding address for a Web site that they have never seen, and possibly not realizing that an accurate address is essential.

Encourage your staff to pass on any feedback they receive about the site, and to suggest new features for it. Front-line staff such as receptionists will be able to help you compile lists of Frequently Asked Questions for the site. Staff photos will help to personalize your site, and if your staff are involved in the development of the Web site, they are more likely to recommend it.

Direct mail

Do not forget to use direct mail to tell people about your site. This might be a straightforward letter telling people about your site and its features when you launch it, or you could send out printed bookmarks or postcards when you add new features or changes, reminding customers to look at your site. If you make these as attractive or humorous as possible, there is more chance they will be retained for future use.

If you are sending a letter, bear in mind that the first impression created by the envelope in which you send your letter is important. Brown paper envelopes are marginally cheaper than white or coloured ones but they look cheap. Window envelopes remind people of bills so although they are practical, they can be off-putting. It is a good idea to check what is printed on your franking machine if you have one, and investigate the possibility of changing the message so that it relates to the mail shot.

Intrigue works well. If you can use intrigue on your envelope or in the first sentence of your letter you will have already involved your reader. This doesn't mean overprinting your envelope with 'Open Now!!! Special Offer Inside!!!' That approach has been over-used. In these days of franking machines and word processors, hand-written envelopes and proper stamps are most likely to attract attention but they are time-consuming to produce.

You will need a definite reason for writing and to avoid a weak letter that simply says you are writing to tell the recipient that you have a Web site. Some reasons for writing might be:

■ an offer or discount only available online;

■ an update about changed or improved Web site content;

■ some free, but valuable, information that is available to download by going to the Web site;

■ a competition or prize draw; for example you could send vouchers with a number or something on them that needs to be matched to another element on the Web site.

Some tips to help you write better direct mail letters

■ Make sure you start with the target's name. If you do not know their name, use another relevant title such as 'Dear walker' or 'Dear worn-out city dweller' instead of 'Dear Sir or Madam'.

■ Use a warm, friendly style. Remember to keep a picture of a typical reader in your mind so that you write a person-alized letter rather than one aimed at 2,000 people, and make sure the style of your letter is in keeping with that of your Web site.

■ Read your letter aloud to make sure it doesn't sound stilted.

■ Try to keep your letter to one side of A4; if it looks longer, recipients may be put off reading it.

■ A PS at the end of the letter will usually attract attention, particularly if it reinforces the sales message; this could be a reminder to look at your Web site.

■ Web site use techniques such as underlining or emboldening to stress important elements of the letter. CAPITAL LETTERS ARE MORE DIFFICULT TO READ.

■ Try to give a strong push to encourage recipients to go to your Web site immediately, such as a bigger discount for online bookings for a specific period of time.

Advertising

The Internet has fuelled the development of two types of advertising. There are now more short, 'directory-style' advertisements and advertisements that are much more integrated with other promotional tools.

The directory-style advertisements are often very short boxes at the end of publications like the Sunday supplements with listings of Web sites, divided according to their specialisation. This is a useful opportunity because you do not need to pay for much space in order to tell people about your Web site. Remember to include a strap-line saying what your site does and how users will benefit, instead of just giving your name and Web site address.

Because you can include almost limitless amounts of information on your Web site, advertisers are now using brief print or television advertisements with the promise of more information on their Web site. They may initiate campaigns offline and then fulfil them online.

A good example of this was a campaign by the Royal Mail. They were in danger of losing revenue from direct-mail shots as more and more organizations use e-mail instead. So they mounted a campaign to encourage more use of direct mail and to explain how it works. Advertisements on television, in magazines and on the London Underground asked a series of multiple-choice questions about attracting and keeping customers. The Royal Mail gave their Web site address as the place to find the answers to their questions.

Other advertisers are building their brands and developing an air of expertise in certain subjects by offering on their Web sites additional information that is not solely connected with the products they advertise. Pampers, makers of a leading brand of nappies, advertised on television without mentioning their product at all. The brief advertisement talked about the different way that toddlers see the world about them and then gave their Web site address for further information, presumably hoping that this would help to reinforce their brand values and create greater product awareness.

If you advertise offline, consider using a different Web site address to your usual one or building a micro-site. This means that you will be able to monitor the effectiveness of your advertising much more closely.

PR activities

When the Internet was first invented, the mere fact of having a Web site was newsworthy enough to guarantee press coverage. Now you will have to work harder, but there are still plenty of publications ready to publish Web site addresses and small features about new sites, especially if they are particularly comprehensive or innovative. You can also generate PR coverage through a success story connected with your Web site or by offering unusual features on it. Using press releases has several advantages.

▓ If your press release gets printed (and you have no guarantee of this: if you want to ensure publication, you need to choose paid advertising instead), you will generate free publicity for your Web site and organization.

▓ Ongoing PR campaigns that lead to periodic coverage help to build your image and business.

▓ Most people find articles far more credible than advertisements. They are also more likely to remember reading about you, so press coverage acts as a very valuable third-party endorsement.

Consider these possible angles for PR activities:

▓ changes and improvements to your site;

▓ new customers or success stories resulting from launch/ development of your site;

▓ launch of new services on your site such as the introduction of online booking;

▓ results from surveys conducted online;

▓ competitions; these might also be connected to a readers' offer;

▓ winning an online award;

▓ launch of a free e-mail newsletter;

▓ a fundraising event you are running on your Web site.

How to write a press release

▓ Make sure you target your release accurately. Write in the style of the publication you are targeting, which might mean writing different style releases for various publications, or slightly changing your story to give it the right slant. If you manage to write in precisely the right tone, some publications will pick up and use your release unchanged and without cutting – sometimes.

▓ Try to answer these questions (they may not all be relevant) in the first paragraph: Who? What? Why? Where? When? How? Editors prefer to cut releases to fit the amount of space available (assuming the story is relevant) so they are usually edited 'bottom up'. This means that the last part of the release is the most likely to be chopped, so do not put important information there; it should be in the first paragraph.

▮ Make the point of the story clear in the first paragraph. Try to encompass the essence of the story in the first sentence to entice the reader to continue reading.

▮ Try to think about the release from the point of view of your target audience and publication, not from your own. Remember that what might be fascinating to you and your directors may not be as interesting to the media.

▮ Do not use complicated language and avoid too much hype (such as using too many words like 'fascinating' or 'exciting'). Be factual and objective. The release should be informative and not read like a 'hard sell' full of PR puff.

▮ If you can think of an appropriate title, include one, but do not try to be too clever – that's the journalist's job! If you write a title, make sure it is short and punchy to grab attention, avoid jargon, and make it really sound like news.

▮ The release should be written in the third person, without using 'I' or 'we'; it should sound as if a journalist has written it, not someone from your staff.

▮ If you are promoting an event, make sure that you have included all relevant details like the time, date, venue and description.

▮ Include the date of the release at the foot of the page.

▮ Remember that your press release is supposed to stimulate editors into wanting to write about or feature your product. To do this, it must be newsworthy, interesting and stimulating.

▮ Make it easy for the journalist to react by putting your contact name, address and telephone/fax numbers at the end of the release. Make sure that the contact details cover office hours and that you give mobile details or another source of information outside office hours, just in case.

▮ It is also a good idea to give your Web site address and the precise URL where your press release, and possibly pictures, can be downloaded, working on the principle that some busy/lazy journalists might be more inclined to use your release if they can simply cut and paste it.

▓ If you have any other important information such as technical data, add this at the end under a general note. If there is a large amount of relevant detail, attach it as an appendix.

▓ A good tip is to read through the information you have written. If a likely reaction to the release could be 'so what?', you will need to rewrite the story or consider another angle.

▓ The timing of your release will be key; bear in mind the sometimes long lead times for publications (up to four months for monthly magazines) and that the media often use releases that tie in to other events or holidays or specific dates. For example, they are always looking for new angles on the usual themes of Valentine's Day and Christmas.

▓ Try to limit your press release to one side of A4, preferably typed using double spacing and wide margins so the copy is easy for journalists to edit. They write notes in the margins and amend the copy in the spaces and then hand it on to someone else to typeset, so if you do not leave enough space they will have to retype the release. That might mean they will not bother and your release will not be published.

▓ Use a good clear font that is easy to read, and make it clear that your press release is a press release. Say so at the top of the page.

▓ Try to avoid sending pages of densely typed information and do not waste money on expensive folders and presentations. The release and its content are most important.

Opinions on whether or not you should chase journalists are mixed. It is certainly a good idea to try to identify which journalists are the most appropriate for your release and to address it directly to them.

Some people find it productive to telephone journalists to find out if they would be interested in a story and to 'pitch' it to them in advance, or to meet with them to give them more detailed briefings. Others make a habit of calling journalists after they should have received the release to find out if they need any additional information and to encourage them to use the release. Some journalists will regard this as 'pestering' and it will not work.

Whatever you do, avoid the temptation of calling with the lame excuse of 'wondering if you got the press release we sent?' The postal system (or e-mail) is too efficient for that excuse to sound anything other than amateur.

One of the disadvantages of PR activities is that you rarely know whether a release has been published unless you actually see it. Few journalists will call up to ask for more information or to tell you that they are going to use your release. Even when they do, there is the risk that the piece will get chopped at the last minute in favour of more important or exciting news. If knowing that you have got some coverage is important to you, it is worth contracting a press clippings service.

Do not forget to target the growing list of e-newsletters and online press resources (there are more details of these in chapter 12).

ONLINE PROMOTIONAL ACTIVITIES

It makes sense to use the Internet to promote your Web site, since your principal target market will be people who are already online.

Search engines

One of the most obvious methods of promoting your site is to register with the major search engines, since this is one of the main ways in which users will find your site. However, you cannot be certain that this will be successful, and need to bear in mind that links and a good, memorable domain name are at least as important.

The name 'search engine' is often used interchangeably to describe actual search engines and 'directories', even though they are not the same. The main difference lies in the way that listings are compiled. Unless there is a need to be very specific, throughout this book they are referred to as 'search engines'.

Some of the more famous so-called search engines such as www.yahoo.com are actually directories. These are compiled by humans who either write short reviews of sites or base listings on short descriptions of sites submitted by site owners. Because they rely on humans, and due to the sheer number of sites submitted to them, it can sometimes take several months before your site appears in the listings – if at all.

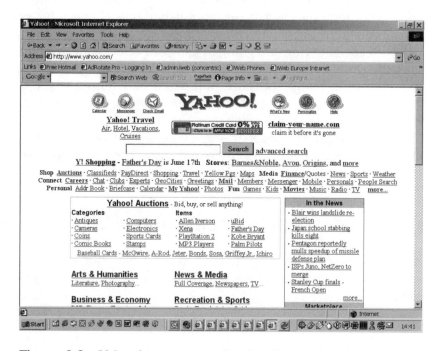

Figure 8.2 Yahoo! is an example of a ***directory*** rather than a search engine, compiled by humans

Search engines such as www.hotbot.com create their listings automatically. They 'crawl' the Web, scanning sites and pages to compile listings. Listings are determined by elements such as page titles and body copy.

If you change the pages of your Web site, search engines will eventually find the changes affecting the listing, whereas directories are unlikely to be affected by changes, unless you tell them.

There are three main elements to search engines:

▨ A 'spider' or 'crawler' is the part that visits sites to read them and follow links.

■ The 'index' or 'catalogue' contains the information found by the spider (it can sometimes take a while for the information to get indexed).

■ Each search engine then has its own special software that sifts through the index and determines the rank of Web sites in their listings. This is why your Web site will be ranked differently by different search engines. Some search engines also index pages more frequently than others.

Figure 8.3 Hotbot is a *search engine* whose listings are compiled automatically

Some search engines combine several techniques, using humans and automatic crawlers. www.askjeeves.com uses a variety of methods. It shows sites reviewed by its human editorial team, includes sites that previous users have found answers on (it calls this a 'popularity' search) and then it uses meta-searching to ask the same question of other search engines like Yahoo! and Altavista.

Criteria for accepting sites on www.askjeeves.com are strict. They only include sites with good, up-to-date content that is unbiased and free to users without registration. This means that although Askjeeves reviews and lists sites much more quickly than some of the other search engines, it only accepts about 20 per cent of all sites submitted.

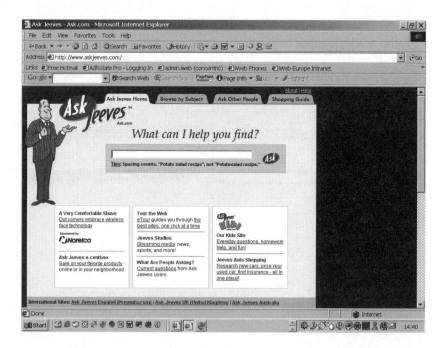

Figure 8.4 Askjeeves is really a combination of directory and search engine, and also uses other methods to compile its search findings

At present in the United Kingdom most listings on search engines and directories are free, although most of them offer advertising opportunities such as a banner advertisement on the search results page for certain keywords.

Because it can take so long to get listed (due to the rapid growth of the Internet and backlog of sites to be reviewed and catalogued), some search engines now offer a paid-for 'express submission' service. Yahoo! charges around $199 in the United

States for its seven-day express service, but there is still no guarantee that they will accept your site and they are thought to accept only around 10 per cent of the sites submitted to them.

It is becoming the norm in the United States to pay to have your site placed on a search service. A further development of the paid-for-placement scenario is that some US operators now also charge site owners a fee for every click-through to their site, usually around 5p per click-through. This may sound very reasonable if it guarantees visitors to your site, but some search engines are going one step further and effectively auctioning high placements in listings to the highest bidder.

If you want to promote your site internationally, you should consider submitting your site to each national version of the search engine, as they do not automatically take the sites from their US or UK partners. It can also help to have a domain name that is relevant to other countries.

You can find more information about how each search engine or directory works by going to their 'help' pages. If you look at the foot of most search engines they have an 'add a site' link, leading to a simple form for submission. Sites such as www. searchenginewatch.com also contain useful information.

Although search engines work in different ways, most of them determine the relevancy of Web sites using similar criteria. These are some of the elements they look for:

■ Pages with keywords appearing in their title are more relevant than others.

■ Pages where the keywords appear near the top of the page, in the headline or first paragraphs are more relevant.

■ The content of the page is important; pages that mention the keywords more frequently and within their true context are likely to achieve a higher ranking.

■ Other criteria include 'link popularity', which is used to some extent by all the search engines to determine how sites should be ranked. The link popularity of your site is determined by the number of Web sites that link to it. You can find out who is linking to your site by using www. linkpopularity.com.

▓ Meta tags are important for some search engines. When they were first developed, some Web site owners repeated key words many times in order to increase their rank in the listings. This is called search engine spamming and most search engines now penalize sites that do this.

Tips to improve your rankings

You will need to identify relevant keywords for search engine registration, and to use them on your site. These should be at least two words long; focusing on just one word will mean that you are in enormous competition with many other sites, but choosing two will increase the relevancy of your site in many searches.

For example, the word 'hotel' will return thousands of sites, where the words 'London hotels' will narrow down the search. However, there will still be many listings for these two key words so words such as 'central' and/or 'town-house', and/or 'budget' might be added.

Search engines cannot read tables in the same way as they are seen on the page. They break the tables in such a way that keywords may be pushed lower down the page. The only solution to this problem is to use meta tags, although not all search engines use them.

If you use image-map links instead of text links you will find that some search engines will not follow the links to pages beyond the home page, which are often the most relevant. One way of counteracting this is to include a site map page with text links to all areas of your Web site. Ensure that you include plenty of good internal links on your site.

Some people use automated programs to submit their sites to the search engines. Some of them are very good. However, the most important search engines respond better to manual submission, which is often the only way to convey the particular nuances and specialities of a site.

The complexities of search engine submission have led to the growth of an army of consultants who claim to be able to improve your chances of a high ranking in the listings. Most of them use very similar techniques to the ones mentioned here, which take as much time as skill and really depend on your intimate knowledge of your customers and how their minds work, to instinctively know what keywords they will search on. Do bear in mind that it can take up to three months before your submitted pages appear in some search engine listings.

If you are tempted to use a 'Web optimization consultancy' why not search for one with various search engines? Presumably if they are really good at their job, their site will be placed at the top of the list.

Once your site is listed, do not assume it will always appear within the listings in the same place. You will need to keep checking it and resubmitting from time to time.

Be aware that search engines are only one of the ways by which people will find you. Search engines list only around 30 per cent of all Web sites in existence.

Reciprocal links

Part of the power of the Internet is the way that so many sites are linked together so that users can follow particular threads to find almost endless information on the subjects they are interested in. Arranging reciprocal links between your site and others is another cost-free way of promoting your site and adding value.

Use the main search engines to look for sites connected to your type of business or destination. Try to think of the keywords your customers might use to find your site.

Use the results and look at the top ten or twenty sites on the list to find the ones that do not compete directly with your site. It is a good idea to go to several search engines and repeat this process. It is naturally best to try to link with sites that offer added value to your users, and to link with complimentary rather than competing sites. It shouldn't cost you anything to do this.

You will need to decide whether you are going to place the links at relevant points within your text and pages, or to group them all together in one part of the site like a directory. It usually seems most natural and appropriate to put the links in context by placing them within the main body of your site. If you do decide to make a special directory, however, you could also invite more submissions from other sites and agree on more reciprocal links with other Webmasters.

Try to think of all the extra information you think your site users would benefit from having, and research the relevant sites. Do not provide links to sites you have not checked out, because your users will see links as a kind of recommendation from you. If your links are irrelevant or inappropriate they might start to doubt the other services you offer. Keep checking the links from time to time to make sure they still exist, and invite feedback from users about your existing links and their suggestions for new ones.

Contact all the sites you would like to link to, giving a brief description of what your site does and the kind of users you target, and ask if they will consider reciprocal links. You will have very limited control over whether they bother to link to you or not, so in some cases you might have to make difficult decisions about whether to provide a link to a site that does not want to link to you or that wants to charge you for doing so. A good general rule of thumb is to simply ask how important the other site is to your customers and if you need to provide the link to offer a complete service.

When you do offer a link to another site, do not just link to their home page. Make sure you link to the most appropriate page within their site so that users are not frustrated by having to click several times to get to useful information.

When you create links to other sites, make sure you let their Webmasters know that you have done so and remind them to link to your site, suggesting the most appropriate page on it for their link.

You might like to consider linking to sites that are potential competitors or consider paying fees to link to certain sites if they are consistently ranked higher in the search engine listings than you. If they are willing to link to your site as well, it could mean that you can indirectly benefit from their higher search engine ranking.

Participate in an affiliate programme

If you are looking for ways to increase the number of people using and buying from your site, many others are doing the same. An affiliate programme is similar to providing a link, but it gives you the opportunity to earn money from the link and possibly improve the services you offer your customers at the same time. Let's say that you have a site promoting a particular destination. You could become an affiliate for a guide-book publisher and link to their site so that every time one of your users goes to the publisher's site and buys a guide book, you will earn a small commission.

Sites like www.tradedoubler.com operate to make the connections between different Webmasters looking to participate in affiliate programmes. There are different commission structures for 'clicks, leads and sales'. Whether you look at developing a fairly formal affiliate system or more casual one with other Webmasters you know, it is a good way of developing your site content and possibly earning some money at the same time as building the number of unique users for your site.

Signature file

More and more communication is now happening by e-mail. Every time you send an e-mail you have a free opportunity to promote your site and your business by including a 'signature file'. You might have seen these at the end of other people's e-mails: a simple sentence or two describing what they do, together with their contact details.

To add a signature file to all your e-mails all you need to do is to set this up within your e-mail program. In Outlook Express, this means going to 'tools', choosing 'options' and then 'signatures'.

Your signature file should be six lines or less, and it is best to keep it to no more than 65 characters wide so that it can be viewed in almost all e-mail programs. Your signature file should include the following:

▨ your name, organization/company and contact information including address and phone numbers;

▨ your Web site and e-mail address;

▨ a brief description of your product or services.

Since it is easy to change your signature file, you might want to adapt it from time to time, in keeping with any changes to your Web site or online promotion you are running.

Two other methods of promoting your site online include the use of e-newsletters and viral marketing. These are both described in more detail in chapter 10.

MONITORING THE EFFECTIVENESS OF YOUR SITE

You have the opportunity to monitor the effectiveness of your site and to find out more about your users. There are several ways of tracking your visitors. Most Internet service providers offer some kind of usage and referrer logs. Another way of getting the information in a more accessible format is to use software such as www.webposition.com or www.webtrendslive.com.

Analysing your log statistics will usually give you an insight into information such as the total number of unique visitors you get, how long they spend on your site and each page, and which search engines are sending you visitors, based on which keywords.

It is more important to know how many unique visitors you get than the total hits, because hits are counted every time a visitor 'requests' information; this can include every page and graphic so it can be a misleading indication. Bad sites with erratic navigation can also generate more hits than good ones, so it is best to be wary of this measurement.

9

ADVERTISING ON THE INTERNET

Developing and promoting your Web site is just one way of attracting more visitors and customers. You can use the Internet as an advertising medium, replacing or combining it with advertising in the press, on the radio or television or in directories.

Any discussion about advertising inevitably leads to repetition of the old adage 'I think half of my advertising is a waste of time; I just do not know which half'. Advertising on the Internet is more accountable. In theory you only pay when someone sees your advertisement. You can track the profile of people who see the ad and even keep an account of who 'clicks' through to your Web site or other information. The reality, however, is not quite so straightforward.

The Internet is a fast-evolving medium, with constant developments. We are only just beginning to learn what works and to move from the limitations of static banner campaigns to the more complicated options of keyword advertising, pop-ups and interstitials.

This chapter covers some of the basics of advertising on the Internet. Advertising agencies, marketing magazines and some of the sites mentioned in chapter 12 will help you keep up to date with further developments. Search engines also carry quite comprehensive information about advertising on their Web sites. Although much of this is specific to each search engine, this information usually acts as a useful introduction to advertising on the Internet.

Marketing is essentially about client or customer acquisition. Advertising can be a good way to initiate a dialogue with potential new customers because it enables you to make contact with customers and people you have not met. It will help you to develop a customer base when you have no idea who or where your potential customers are.

Advertising makes them aware of you and encourages them to show interest in what you have to offer. Once they start doing that you can begin to identify and profile them and to work out what you must do to make certain they buy from you and not your competition.

Advertising will help you acquire new customers, but you almost certainly need to take a multi-channel approach. This means using a variety of media, messages and promotional activities to make an impact. It also means that you should look to develop an ongoing relationship with your clients. Internet marketers are increasingly talking about the lifetime value of a customer. That means repeat selling, cross-selling and encouraging your customer base to generate referrals for you.

Do not make the mistake of forgetting all the lessons you have learnt through more traditional forms of advertising. All the 'rules' about positioning, monitoring, negotiating to get the best deals and conveying the most appropriate messages to your target audience at the right time are still true.

Advertising usually has either tactical or strategic objectives. Strategic advertising is concerned with creating an awareness of products and services, developing new markets and building your identity and image. It takes a more long-term view and needs even more careful planning than tactical advertising. Strategic advertising tends to be more expensive because it needs to build awareness over a longer period of time and it is harder to monitor its direct effectiveness.

Tactical advertising is aimed at specific market segments and persuading them to go to a particular place or buy a certain service, sometimes at a particular time. Tactical advertising takes a more short- to-medium-term view. The Internet is especially useful in this role. There are not many advertising media that allow you to notice that you have not sold all the tickets for a concert that evening and to have a last-minute campaign up and running within an hour, which you can then stop as soon as the tickets are sold. The Internet does – at a very affordable price.

BENEFITS OF ADVERTISING ON THE INTERNET

Immediacy

The Internet enables you to respond to changes in record time. In an industry like tourism that relies on the promotion of services that are essentially 'perishable' (if you do not sell your hotel rooms for tonight by this evening, you will not get another chance to do so; they will have 'perished' and you will have lost revenue), the Internet's immediacy is invaluable. You can mount tactical campaigns as soon as you know that you have surplus capacity and change both the message and frequency of your advertising to suit external factors.

Targeting

You can book advertisements that reach very carefully targeted audiences. In theory you could book ads to be seen at particular times of the day, or on certain days of the week. You can decide where the consumers should be or what type of profile they should have, all the way down to the country or region they access the Internet from.

One of the most popular and highly targeted methods is to advertise on keywords with the search engines. They are then seen only by people searching for a particular keyword or key phrase such as 'gay pubs in Edinburgh'.

Every time a user types in your chosen keyword into a search, your advertisement will appear. This means that it appears on the search results page at exactly the time when a user is searching for information on that topic.

Flexibility

Advertising on the Internet is more flexible than most other media, in terms of changing messages or targets and the speed with which you can put together a campaign. You can change the message or other elements of your campaign while it is actually running, once you have decided what works best for you. This chance to 'practise-and-refine' is probably one of the greatest benefits of Internet advertising.

Directness

If customers are interested in an online advertisement, they can click on it to receive more information immediately, and can also link to a booking mechanism. Consumers can be taken straight to the point of sale and encouraged to book or buy right away. They would normally have to move through several stages of awareness until they were persuaded to buy, and at every stage of promotion there would be the danger that they might simply forget to buy from you or lose interest. On the Internet, advertising does not just help to build brands and awareness, but can ultimately take a consumer from initial information to a confirmed booking.

Cost savings

Thanks to this interactivity and ease of processing bookings or purchases, there are potentially large savings on customer service costs, as well as the relatively low cost of advertising on the Internet. It is also easier to keep customers informed of any changes to their bookings by using automated e-mails. Imagine the case of a holiday company promoting tours to an area hit by a natural disaster. They would be able to inform customers whether it is still safe to travel, allowing the company to take a proactive and reassuring stance and to pre-empt a flurry of cancellations.

Easy-to-monitor responses

You will be able to find out exactly how many people have seen your advertisement and how many clicked on it. If you place advertisements with different messages on different sites, you can also evaluate which ones work best.

The Internet can also act as a response and further-information mechanism for other forms of advertising. For example, a radio advertisement is usually too short to convey complicated information, but there is sufficient time to give out the address of a Web site that contains more details. You can also develop special Web sites or micro-sites and only use those addresses through other forms of advertising. This will enable you to use the Internet to measure the effectiveness of other offline advertising.

In summary, Internet advertising can be used to:

▓ identify qualified sales leads;

▓ generate and respond to requests for information;

▓ build a relationship with customers;

▓ help you to develop a profile of customers.

BANNER ADVERTISEMENTS

The most common form of online advertising is the 'banner ad'. These rectangular-shaped boxes are usually placed at the top of the Web page like a banner headline in a newspaper, although they can appear in other positions. They generally measure 468 × 60 pixels; this size has become more or less standard to make it easier to develop campaigns.

Consumers click on banners to get more information, usually being taken to the advertiser's Web site. Because the banner is small, advertising messages are usually short and to the point, with a simple call to action. Many use humour or extremely straightforward messages. Banners can be used to build brands and awareness or to take the user right through to the point of sale. For example, a banner ad might ask the question 'table tonight?' and then click through to a site that takes online last-minute restaurant reservations.

Banner ads are developing to include 'rich media', offering the opportunity to add animations or short video clips to attract attention. Video banners are a strong branding tool since they can combine the power of TV advertising with the targeting of the Internet and therefore drive higher numbers of consumers to Web sites. The downside of this is that they take longer to download, and the customer may move on from the site before seeing them. In other cases, using the latest whiz-bang technology requires users to install special software to view such banners, which minimizes the potential audience of the campaign. It still pays to 'keep it simple'.

INTERSTITIALS

The Web is still a huge experimental zone and interstitials are evidence of this. Interstitial advertisements are displayed in between Web pages. This is similar to turning the page of a magazine and being faced with a double page advert that you have to see before you turn the page again.

On the Web, when you click on a new link, a Web site will often load an advert first before taking you on to the page requested. In some cases you have to click on a button to continue loading the next page. The main benefit to advertisers is that it is almost impossible to ignore the advertisement, but interstitials are also more likely to irritate Internet users.

POP-UP ADS

A pop-up ad literally pops up as a new window with an advertising message on some Web sites. Some sites use them on a limited basis because of their visibility and generally higher click-through rates. However, the down side is that the window often obscures part of the page, thereby annoying the user.

A company called iWeb has developed a simple advertising technology called iNotes. It is a non-intrusive form of pop-up advertisement that is controlled by the Internet service provider, and means that Internet users can see communications and occasional advertising messages regardless of the site they are looking at. The system is in use by the United Kingdom's largest ISP, Freeserve.

BOOKING ADVERTISING

You can buy advertising direct from Web site owners, but it is likely to be a time-consuming process to find relevant sites. It is even more likely that there are sites which could be invaluable to you that you have not even heard of. It does make sense to use a new-media agency, whether they are an off-shoot of a traditional advertising agency or a specialist one.

Before you start to work with a new agency, make sure you ask them for some case studies of successful campaigns they have already worked on and some client references. They may understand advertising, but do they have a track record of running campaigns on the Internet?

You will need to follow the same process for setting up an online campaign as you would offline, but it should be much quicker. You will need to brief the agency and agree concrete objectives so that either you or the agency can develop the right creative treatment and then the agency can book space. It is possible to develop a new campaign and actually have it up and running within a few hours, but a couple of weeks would be a more realistic time-frame.

Campaigns can be reviewed on a weekly basis, or more frequently if you prefer, so you can adapt the message and creative treatment while the campaign is actually running. The agency you use should compile statistics to help you see how the advertising is running so you can decide what is and isn't working for you.

These statistics are compiled using 'ad servers'. An ad server controls the process of transferring an advertisement to the Web site where it will be seen and enables you to get ad server statistics. These will show how many impressions have been served or presented, their click-through rates, which messages or banners have worked best and which sites have been most successful. Make sure you are provided with the login details of the reporting software to enable you to track the success of your campaign

Advertisements are sold based on a number of 'impressions', usually by the thousand. An impression is a page view, so that each time a surfer sees a page, it counts as an impression. This means that if you buy 50,000 impressions, your ad will be seen 50,000 times. Advertising rates are quoted as CPMs (the cost per thousand impressions).

A more recent development gaining popularity is to charge by performance, most commonly expressed as CPC (cost per click). The Easy Everything chain of Internet cafés (owned by the same group as EasyJet) charges around 50p per click. This means that even if you run a campaign with 1,000,000 impressions and only one person clicks on the ad, you only pay 50p, although there are usually minimum charges.

Recent research undertaken by Engage (an Internet specialist advertising firm) has shown that even though users may not initially click on an ad, they are more likely to go to an advertised site within a short period of time, proving that the Internet also acts as a powerful brand-building medium.

Just as you would expect to pay more for an advertisement for a visitor attraction close to a magazine article about 'where to take the children at half term', you will also pay more for targeted ads in special positions within a Web site. Run-of-site ads should be cheaper, which means you can perhaps afford to book more impressions and experiment a little to find what kind of sites and positions work.

You can expect to pay around £15 CPM for run-of-site ads (sometimes also called a general rotation campaign) and around £40 to £50 for more targeted ads. You can expect results for targeted ads to be up to four times better than run-of-site ads. There is usually a minimum cost, often around £1,000 to £2,000.

The travel section of Freeserve's portal site, one of the busiest in the United Kingdom, is consistently sold out of banner advertising, which will also drive up the CPM.

The 'click-through' is the percentage of people who see an advertisement and click on it, so it is a very tangible way of measuring the response rate of a campaign. 'Average' click-through rates were initially around 2 or 3 per cent, partly thanks to the novelty factor. They are now more likely to be around 0.5 per cent, although this will depend on the type of product or service being sold, the positioning of the ad. and the creative message.

If you do want to book your own banner ads directly, take a look at sites like www.lycos.co.uk that offer advertisers the opportunity to buy and create their own banner online. First-time advertisers might welcome the chance to use one of their banner design templates that can be tailored and customized to suit their needs. There is no need to download anything; all that advertisers have to do is click on a 'banner master' and then click to add their company name and other details. A flat fee is charged for this service, ranging from around £16 up to about £40.

When you book an ad on a particular site, don't be surprised if you don't always see it when you go to that Web site. Ads are often served in rotation with others unless you have specified that you want yours to be displayed almost constantly, which would be more akin to sponsorship and subject to more detailed negotiation (and higher prices!).

When you book advertising do not be tempted to use sites just because they have high traffic. You will need to ensure that the site's visitors have the right profile for your service. You should be able to ask the site for audited traffic reports, which are now produced by companies such as Nielsen Netratings and Jupiter MMXI. You will find that advertising rates are higher on Web sites with a niche market even though they may have lower traffic.

Be wary of thinking that sites with the highest number of impressions are always the best. Sometimes, badly designed sites have a higher number of impressions because of the need to navigate so much around the site to find relevant information.

Because the Internet is such a flexible advertising medium, avoid booking too many impressions at once. You can under-take test advertising first of all, booking minimum numbers of impressions so you can gauge the response to different creative messages, positions and sites.

One key benefit of online advertising is that you can measure click-through rates and monitor the success of your campaign, but be aware that this is not the only means by which your customers might respond to the advertisement. An advertise-ment for a hotel may act as a trigger for a guest to undertake further research, looking up further details about the hotel or destination on other sites, before actually making a booking.

Since the booking is as likely to be by telephone as online, you might not be able to trace the original prompt for the booking, unless your receptionist always asks how people heard about you.

Tips to improve banner advertisements

▦ Make sure the concept for the banner ad is in keeping with your overall brand and any other advertising you are running.

▦ Make sure the banner message is relevant to your target audience. Show that you recognize their specific needs.

▦ Be clear about what you are trying to achieve: to build awareness of your product or service? To draw more customers to your site? To encourage people to make direct bookings with you? Whatever your objectives, keep them in mind. There is only limited space on a banner ad so you will not have room to try to fulfil more than one objective.

▦ Some advertisers 'con' the public by making statements or offers that encourage users to click through to their site but then disappoint the user because they are not real offers. It is not worth increasing click-through rates if users do not become customers. Make sure that your banner headline promise is fulfilled by the information on the next page that you take users to.

▦ The banner is a very small space and needs to grab attention and push the reader into action. The best way of doing this is to keep the message and creative treatment very simple and direct. You can offer more complete information at the next stage, when the user has clicked through to your site.

▦ You will probably find that you have several messages you want to convey. Avoid this temptation and choose just one really strong message.

▦ Banners that have the words 'click here' consistently perform better than those that do not.

▓ Once you have got consumers to click through your banner ad to the next stage, make sure you offer an incentive or strong reason for them to stay with you and move to the next stage: buying from you or making a booking.

▓ Think carefully about where surfers are taken when they click on an advertisement. Do not send them simply to the home page of your Web site so that they have to click further to get relevant information. Ensure the page they are taken to is the most relevant, perhaps in a special area of your site, or on a micro-site.

E-MAIL AS A
PROMOTIONAL TOOL

This chapter looks at various ways in which the Internet can help you to develop a relationship with your customers, to build awareness of your services and encourage loyalty so that they return to you again and again.

Research indicates that the main reason for people initially going online is to be able to use e-mail, with entertainment and information via the Internet coming second and third. E-mail is a powerful and popular medium, and has two added benefits: it is extremely cheap and very direct. It arrives directly on the desktop of the person you are contacting, often only minutes after you have sent it.

The ability to replace 'snail mail' (postal) direct marketing campaigns with e-mail is an important development for marketers. It will help you to build relationships with your customers and create brand awareness as well as increasing sales.

The main difference between direct mail by e-mail rather than post is that e-mail typically costs less than half as much (taking into consideration the costs of obtaining names, putting together a mailing and distribution costs). It can produce results that are from two to five times better. The set-up and response times are also much faster; you could generate results within 24 hours.

The National Ice Centre in Nottingham uses an e-mail database of regular visitors to fill surplus capacity. This approach was successful the very first time it was used. On that occasion, the last-minute repositioning of some spotlights cleared previously obscured views for a concert and meant that there were some extra tickets released on the day of the actual performance. E-mails were sent to 700 people who had registered their details on the Web site and within an hour all 50 extra tickets had been sold. This speed of activity and response would be almost impossible with any other promotional tool.

E-mailings are more versatile than they might initially seem. You can send text messages as plain e-mail text or include HTML so that your mailing looks like a page from a Web site. You can also include other pictures or even animation and video clips. One of the most popular tactics is to send out a regular newsletter, described later in this chapter.

You can send bulk e-mails from your own computer but some Internet Service Providers will block them if you try to send the same message to a lot of different recipients so you might need to break up your mailing list into smaller 'chunks'. If you are considering a very big mailing it can make sense to use a reputable mailing house instead so that they can deal with tracking and analysing responses and 'undelivered' messages. If you are using your own database, a mailing house can help you to update and clean it.

Alternatively, you might decide to buy in a mailing list. If you do, ensure it is from a reputable company or broker and the names on it are 'opt in'. This means that recipients have agreed to receive mailings.

Sending unsolicited and untargeted e-mails to lists of people you do not know is called 'spamming'. The plus side to it is that it costs practically nothing to do and there is always the tiniest chance that you might get a positive response. However, it is far more likely that response rates will be very, very low and you will certainly irritate people (if you 'spam' you might get 'flamed', which means receiving angry e-mails!). Some Internet Service Providers will cancel their services to known 'spammers'.

A better alternative is to use 'opt-in' e-mail and develop your own list and database of people who are at least interested in what you have to say. Response rates will be higher if you build your own carefully targeted lists.

There are several ways of building your own lists:

▓ Encouraging your Web site users to request additional information by completing a short form with their details. If you do this, make sure the information you ask for is very short and to the point.

▓ Giving away something such as a free guidebook and asking people to fill in their details on your Web site. As you do this, you have an opportunity to ask if recipients would like to receive information from you from time to time. You will also need to offer them information about how to remove their details from your mailing list at some point in the future if they wish.

▓ By running an online survey or competition and requesting permission from participants to e-mail them from time to time.

As you build your list you should always make it clear what you are planning to do with your e-mail address list. You will encourage more people to participate if you make a promise that you will not give away or sell your e-mail address list to anyone else and that it will be for your use only. There are more details about privacy and the Data Protection Act at the end of this chapter.

PERMISSION MARKETING

One of the current buzz terms in Web promotion is 'permission marketing', used most extensively by Internet marketing 'guru' Seth Godin. At its simplest, permission marketing means asking your customers to agree to receive mailings and information from you so that you can build up a relationship and sell to them. Of course, customers are not always exactly aware that this is what is happening, and more subtle techniques may be used! Another definition is that permission marketing encourages consumers to participate in a long-term, interactive marketing campaign in which they are rewarded in some way for paying attention to increasingly relevant messages.

This means that once a customer has made contact with you via your Web site (or another means) and given you their e-mail address, you have an opportunity to communicate with them. Most of us want to benefit from better information and services, and can understand that suppliers will be more likely to provide them to us if they know who we are and what we want. Various studies have shown that Internet users are prepared to give details about their needs, interest and profiles – but only so long as they receive useful and relevant information in return.

Some people will need an incentive; it might be as straight-forward as the promise of improved service but could equally be more tangible in terms of a discount, some form of voucher or added-value deal. One of the results of permission marketing is increased trust in certain services and products, and the beginning of a relationship between consumer and supplier.

There is a condition to asking for such information and data: if you do request it, you must ensure you use it and that consumers do see some improvements; otherwise you have broken their trust and disappointed them. At this point consumers are likely to withdraw their permission to communicate with them and stop buying from you.

Developing a longer-term relationship with your clients so that they come back to you may not seem so appropriate if you are an individual hotel in a remote location that guests visit only occasionally. But think of the wider implications of that visit if it is successful. It is not only the original guests who will come back to you if their stay and booking experience was positive and memorable in some way, but also their friends and relatives.

This approach can also be appropriate for clusters of similar-minded organizations such as a tourist board covering a wider area. The effort of gathering data on visitors and their needs is usually rewarded because the costs, time and benefits can be shared between several organizations.

The key benefits of permission marketing are that:

■ You know that people are positively interested in your service so you are effectively dealing with customers who are pre-qualified, and more likely to buy from you. Companies in the United States claim response rates of between 5 and 17 per cent.

■ Because they have agreed to receive information from you, customers anticipate your mailings and, you may hope, look forward to hearing from you.

■ The messages you send can be more relevant and personalized because you are able to gather a certain amount of information from potential recipients.

It would be unrealistic to expect potential customers to provide details and information about themselves without some form of reward or incentive. If a consumer offers information about what they want, like or dislike, you should be in a position to provide it. You will need to offer better service, special offers and, ultimately, a more long-term relationship and trust.

This means taking a long-term approach:

■ offering the consumer an incentive to be on your mailing list;

■ providing only relevant information and building their trust;

■ reinforcing the incentive to ensure that the consumer continues to want to receive your information;

■ offering further incentives to obtain more information about them and to continue to sell to them.

Bear in mind that with e-mail the recipient effectively pays to receive your mailing so you should respect the fact that at some point they might wish to unsubscribe from your mailings. Remember too that some people see their inbox as more personal than a letterbox because it is dedicated to them and right in front of their nose.

If you offer relevant and timely information in a newsletter it is likely that recipients may wish to recruit new subscribers on your behalf. You can actively encourage other people to pass on your details and to become part of the same network so that you have access to a much broader market.

DEVELOPING AN E-NEWSLETTER

An e-newsletter is an excellent way to communicate with your customers because it is such a cheap and direct means. The Internet makes it as easy to send a direct message to 1,000 people as it is to one person.

Certain conventions have developed surrounding the format for newsletters. These have evolved to ensure e-newsletters are easy to read and use. It is worth sticking to the following format.

Try to keep your text to about 55 characters per line, so that almost all e-mail programmes can display it without changing the format. This will avoid some recipients seeing broken lines and strange layouts.

The following is an accepted format with suggested order of contents:

NEWSLETTERS

Title of your newsletter

Include a short one-line description of what you do and benefits to your customers
Your Name and E-mail Address

- -

Welcome to '*Title of your newsletter*'
You are receiving this newsletter because you requested
it. We hope you will continue to want to read it,
but if you would like to unsubscribe at any time, please see the
instructions at the end of this newsletter.

- -

In this issue:

List of contents – for example:

- Sponsorship notice
- Feature article
- Information about new products or services
- Guest column

■ Classified ads
■ Subscribe/unsubscribe information

- -

Leave one or two blank lines before you start the
first paragraph so it is easier to read

- -

You can also break up your newsletter
with 'did you know' style tips or information
about something you offer for free

- -

Copyright information

- -

Concluding messages

■ Please pass this newsletter on (encouraging recipients to recommend
  it to others)
■ How to subscribe
■ How to unsubscribe

- -

Your signature file
Your name/company
Your e-mail address
Your Web address (it is important to add the 'http://' prefix)
A short description of your products or services and how they benefit
your customers

- -

PROMOTING YOUR NEWSLETTER

When people first subscribe to your newsletter, send them a
short message to thank them and tell them again how to unsubscribe if they wish and how to refer new readers to you.

Do not make your readers scroll through several lines of
e-mail addresses until they get to the main body copy. Be careful

not to inadvertently give away the details of your mailing list. Make sure you copy all the e-mail addresses to the 'BCC' field, which stands for 'Blind Carbon Copy', so that the recipients do not see each other's e-mail addresses.

You will encourage more people to sign up to your e-newsletter or allow you to keep their details on your mailing list if you state that you comply with the Data Protection Act and if you publish a privacy statement within your site (see chapter 11 for an example of a privacy statement).

DATA PROTECTION AND PRIVACY ISSUES

There is no doubt that Internet users are becoming increasingly aware that companies hold more and more data about them, which is not always used as ethically as it should be. You certainly need to be aware of the Data Protection Act and to be able to reassure your Web site users and e-mail recipients that you aim to protect their privacy.

The Data Protection Act 1998 came into effect on 1 March 2000. You risk heavy fines and penalties if you fail to comply with it. The new Act is especially applicable to those doing business electronically, but it applies equally to any business maintaining or using information on individuals (as opposed to limited companies and the like).

You should register under the Act if there is any possibility of your holding any information on individuals that may (either on its own or when linked to other details in your possession or control) enable them to be identified or contacted. The cost is around £35 a year. You can initially register your company by telephoning the Data Protection Registrar on 01625 545700. It is particularly important to tell the DPR if you intend taking enquiries online using the Internet.

The Act states that if any information you use includes information on one or more human beings, you must ensure that:

▓   The information is used fairly and lawfully. This means, for example, that you cannot use a database to market products from other companies in the same group as yours, or even new products for your company unless you have each person's consent. Also, if you buy mailing lists it is especially important to get a warranty that the information has been obtained legally and can be used for the purposes for which you have purchased it.

▓ You only keep the minimum amount of information necessary for your purposes.

▓ Information you hold on anyone is used only in accordance with their consent (which can be withdrawn at any time).

▓ The information is accurate and, where necessary, is kept up to date and deleted when no longer required.

▓ You keep the information safe and secure at all times.

▓ You do not transfer the information outside Europe unless to a county where there are adequate data protection laws (the United States and Canada do not have such laws, for example).

VIRAL MARKETING

Yet another Internet buzz word, viral marketing is basically a way of providing your customers with information or an offer that is so good that they want to forward it to their friends. Thus they become your very own unpaid sales force.

Viral marketing is all the more powerful because it is effectively a way of triggering word-of-mouth publicity, which is the best form of promotion and the one we all find most credible. We trust our friends and their recommendations, and when a friend forwards an e-mail or some information to us, we intrinsically believe they have selected us as a relevant and appropriate recipient for that particular piece of information. We read and digest such messages more avidly than any others.

The power of viral marketing is that it has a life of its own. Like the less pleasant 'bug' version, it grows exponentially, taking advantage of rapid multiplication to pass on your marketing message to millions. It is very much a grassroots medium, so messages can be received by anyone with e-mail access.

However, like the 'bug' version it also has a less positive side: it cannot be controlled. This means that there is no guarantee that your message will really be passed on and also no guarantee that your viral marketing message will not get hijacked and somehow turned against you.

A positive example of how viral marketing can work is www.hotmail.com, one of the first free Web-based e-mail services. Hotmail gives away free e-mail addresses that can be used from anywhere in the world. Their service is simple: users sign up and can then check their e-mail messages when not at home or in their office.

Each free message has a short tagline attached to it: 'Get your private, free e-mail at http://www.hotmail.com'. So with virtually no other promotion, hotmail has grown rapidly simply through people e-mailing to their own network of friends, who see the message and then sign up for the service. This brings them to the hotmail Web site and to see the advertisers on that site.

Some of the other best examples of viral e-mails have been short video clips or jokes that get forwarded around the world. Now marketers are trying to use the power of viral marketing to attract new customers to their Web sites and to use their products.

The best viral marketing campaigns are those that at least appear uncontrived but that do the following:

▓ They are easy to forward and of common interest to a vast number of people.

▓ They are usually either emotional, humorous and/or full of very useful information.

▓ They give away something that other people are likely to want or offer information they are likely to want to see. A good example of this is a screen-saver.

Guinness promoted themselves very successfully in the early days of the Internet by offering a free and easy-to-download screen-saver of a glass of Guinness emptying, which was then forwarded from office to office and colleague to colleague until it seemed to appear on desktop computers everywhere.

Competitions and quizzes can help to drive visitors to your site.

Lastminute.com used a simple quiz as a way of generating interest in their Valentine's Day offers. www.officeflirttest.com was a separately branded stand-alone site. Aimed at 25–44-year-old urban professionals, it asked users to answer three pages of multiple-choice questions to determine what type of office flirt they were. This promotion was fully integrated, benefiting from a range of activities to promote the site. A series of 16 SMS-based messages helped to drive traffic to the site and 10,000 'office flirting kits' were also distributed to receptionists across the United Kingdom containing Lastminute.com Valentine postcards and posters. Lastminute.com staff sent information about the site to their friends, hoping they would visit it and pass it on to their friends, who in turn would also forward details of the site. It worked: on the afternoon of its launch, the site had 50,000 page impressions.

E-COMMERCE
OPPORTUNITIES

Travel services are already the largest consumer e-commerce category in the United States, accounting for 30 per cent of all online retail. There is an increasing expectation from consumers that they should be able to buy or make bookings on tourism and leisure Web sites.

In fact, the lack of booking or purchasing facilities is often a major cause of frustration for consumers on many sites. Until now, e-commerce in the tourism and leisure industries has focused on air ticket sales and hotel bookings. This is mainly thanks to the existence of global distribution systems like Sabre, on which it is possible to build and incorporate e-commerce for air tickets and hotels.

Take-up of the e-commerce opportunity has been more limited among attractions, smaller hotels and other leisure operators like fitness centres, but it is forecast to grow rapidly.

Developing a Web site capable of accepting online bookings or acting as a shop-front is potentially complex because of the need to build a suitable 'back-office' system, to develop a secure site and accept online payments.

This chapter is intended to help you consider some of the issues that are involved, but does not attempt to cover them all in detail. You are recommended to seek more detailed technical advice before embarking on the development of an e-commerce site.

If you are keen to accept online bookings you basically have three options:

▊ Work with an established online booking agent who has already developed suitable systems and can incorporate your hotel or attraction into their operations. This means that you potentially benefit from much greater and broader exposure. The downside is that your competitors will be promoted along with you and it is harder to maintain your own identity. You might decide to use this option and one of the other two listed below.

▊ Buy an off-the-shelf software solution. This is usually cheaper and easier than developing your own solution from scratch. Most systems are very comprehensive but more suited to selling products than services. Some of them use templates that can be difficult to tailor to your precise needs. They may look out of place within some sites, and since many of the solutions were first developed in the United States, may have an American slant (the less sophisticated, cheaper ones only accept payment in dollars!).

▊ Develop your own site with the help of a programmer. This will be the most expensive option but in the long run probably the most productive because you will have a tailor-made system that is completely suited to your needs.

Whichever option you choose, it is useful to bear in mind the following:

▊ Setting up an e-commerce site is not just a one-off cost. You will need to commit a budget for its ongoing development and improvement, and bear in mind the costs of accepting credit card payments and so on (see below).

▊ When dealing with e-commerce system suppliers, ask for examples of previous satisfied clients and their contact details. Make sure you speak to them before committing yourself.

▊ If you do decide to commission new, tailor-made software, bear in mind that you will probably need to commit substantial staff time to the project, even if using external consultants. Staff training will be crucial to building consumer confidence. This means making sure they tell customers about the facility and can answer any queries they might have.

■ If you have an important deadline for implementation of the new booking/sales system, include a penalty clause in the contract with your supplier.

■ Make certain that your supplier provides plenty of training and after-care.

■ Make sure you set up methods of monitoring the success of the system and a timescale for doing so.

■ Make sure you test the site thoroughly before starting to promote it. Sites that do not do what they promise are bad enough. If they are promoted as e-commerce sites and do not work, consumers will lose all confidence in them.

In addition to the actual booking system on your site, you will also need to consider two other important issues:

■ how you will accept payment for bookings;

■ how you will make your site secure.

PROCESSING PAYMENT

There are several ways of accepting payment online:

■ By credit card over a secure link; this is set to become the most popular method although not all consumers are ready to use it yet.

■ By credit card over an insecure link; not to be encouraged and very unlikely to be accepted by consumers.

■ By the consumer printing off details and then telephoning or faxing credit card details.

The merchant must first obtain authorization for the charge from the merchant's credit card processing company. Authorization simply means that the card has not been reported stolen and there is sufficient credit on the card. It results in the customer's credit limit being temporarily reduced by the value of the transaction. When the transaction is complete, the amount is transferred to the supplier.

There are two ways in which credit card authorization (that is, checking that the card is not stolen and there is enough credit on the card) can be obtained:

- Manually: you would take details of the booking from the Web server and then request authorization using a point-of-sale terminal provided by the credit card company.

- Automatically: details of the payment are automatically communicated to the credit card processing company computer and authorized online. This option is preferable but costs slightly more.

MAKING YOUR SITE SECURE

Consumers are increasingly aware of the need to make bookings or payments only on secure sites. The main technology used to facilitate this is called SSL or Secure Socket Layer. This means that all communication with the Web server is encrypted or coded so that the credit card information cannot be stolen. When the Web site moves into secure mode using SSL it is usual for the customer to see this is happening. If they use Netscape Navigator as their browser they will see a blue key and blue line and if they use Internet Explorer, a padlock symbol.

Even when you are using SSL technology, the customer's credit card information should be additionally protected once it is stored on the Web server and before it is passed to the booking site. This is usually done either by encrypting the information stored on the server or by using a 'firewall'. This is software that prevents 'trespassers' from stealing information from the server. Some credit card companies insist on their merchants using a firewall.

Finally, you should bear in mind that different laws may apply to e-commerce and booking procedures online to offline. You should consider asking your solicitor to draw up precise terms and conditions for any commerce on your site.

There are still some concerns among consumers about e-commerce. You will need to overcome these before you can encourage them to buy or book online.

The most common concern is about secure payment facilities. Using credit cards online will eventually be an accepted method for most people, but in the meantime offer your customers a range of different ways of paying, including printing off forms that can be faxed to you with their credit card details or tele-phoning.

DEVELOPING A PRIVACY STATEMENT

The other major concern surrounds privacy and the ways in which any information about a consumer might be used in the future. You can overcome this concern by publishing a privacy statement on your site.

A privacy statement can be as simple or complex as you think necessary for your target markets. If you are just asking users of your site to register to receive further information, you will probably need to give them a small incentive to do so (this might be the quality of the information itself) and to explain why you are collecting the data, and what it will and will not be used for. It is a good idea to include an explanation of the benefits to your customers when collecting such information. These benefits might include better services and offers (try to be specific), improved navigation of the site, more personalized services and so on.

However, if you are actually selling on your site you will probably need to offer much more detailed information about your privacy policy. Below are two examples of privacy state-ments; you will need to rewrite them, taking into consideration particular aspects of your own business and Web site. You are recommended to take legal advice in order to draft the most appropriate information. You can see how other companies deal with these issues by looking at some of the leading e-commerce tourism sites such as www.britishairways.com, which includes a 'highlights' privacy policy and a full version. You are not recommended to copy such statements. They have been specially developed for the companies whose sites you see and you would almost certainly be in breach of copyright.

The following two examples could be used as a basis for developing your own statements. Neither of them has been checked by a lawyer. You are strongly advised to take legal advice on this aspect of Web site development.

Short privacy statement

When anyone uses this Web site our Web server automatically creates log files containing technical information about their connection. This includes such things as how long people use the site and what pages they visit but no personally identifiable information is created. We use this technical information to understand how people use this site and to improve the site's content.

If you e-mail us with a request for more information we will record your e-mail address for future mailings. However, we DO NOT make this information available to any other organization. If you wish us to remove your e-mail address from our records, please let us know and we will willingly do so straight away.

Longer, more detailed version of a privacy statement

Your privacy is important to us so we have adopted the following policy, and want to let you know how we use and process your personal information.

We promise that your personal information will only be used in ways that are compatible with this privacy policy.

Every computer connected to the Internet has a domain name and set of numbers known as that computer's IP address, standing for 'Internet Protocol'. When a visitor visits a page from within our Web site, our Web server automatically recognizes that visitor's domain name and IP address. The domain name and IP address reveal nothing personal about you other than the IP address from which you have accessed our site.

We use this information to examine the way visitors use our site in general but do not collect and evaluate this information on individuals or record e-mail addresses of site visitors.

Sometimes we use 'cookies' to see which parts of the site you have visited or customized, and how often you have seen them, so those pages are readily accessible next time you visit the site. This can improve the service we offer you. A cookie is a small piece of data sent to your browser from our Web server and stored on your computer's hard drive. It does not damage your computer system and cannot read information from your hard disk.

If you would prefer not to accept cookies you can change the settings on your browser, and you can also enable your browser to show you when a cookie is being sent. Deciding not to accept cookies might diminish your experience at some sites because some features might not work as intended.

If we ask for your e-mail or postal address, for example, to send you additional information or conduct a survey, we will let you know exactly how we intend to use that information. We would like to assure you that we will not ever sell, rent, or give your e-mail address to anyone else without your prior consent. We will not send you any e-mail that you have not agreed to receive in advance. From time to time we may send you e-mails announcing new services on our Web site but you can choose to remove your details from our mailing list at any time. If you buy something from us/book on our site, we will need to know your name, e-mail address, postal address, credit card number and expiry date, in order to fulfil your order/booking and inform you about its status/progress. We might use this information to notify you of related products and services but will not share it or sell it to anyone else for any reason. Again, you can choose to delete your details at any time.

Our site is protected using Secure Socket Layer technology, which encrypts the payment information you give us, making it unreadable to anyone trying to intercept the information.

Please bear in mind that this site links to many other Web sites and we are not responsible for their privacy policies. Please check with those sites to determine their privacy policy.

If you choose to remove your details from our mailing lists, please notify us and we will do so immediately. To do so, please contact xxxxxxx.

OTHER WAYS TO REASSURE CUSTOMERS

Because e-commerce is still in its early stages of development, you will probably need to find other ways of reassuring customers and Web site users. The following are some of the ways you can do this.

Ensure that you display a list of terms and conditions on your site so customers can see the terms under which you are trading *before* they commit themselves. You can also design your site so that customers have to signify their agreement by clicking on a button before proceeding to the next stage or confirming the transaction.

Use good photographs (preferably optimized so the images are small file sizes and load quickly) so your customers can see exactly what they are booking. This is especially important if your clients are likely to travel a long way to get to you. It will help to build confidence that you really exist, and encourage visitors to make the journey to come to visit or stay with you.

Give as much detail about the services you offer as possible. Consider any possible concerns and questions your customers may have and make sure you include the answers to these on your site. A 'Frequently Asked Questions' section is a good way to do this.

Referring to other satisfied customers or guests will help to reassure potential customers and encourage them to book online. You could also mention the percentage of repeat guests or customers you have and how many of them recommend you to others.

Develop some content that enhances your site and conveys to users the idea that you want to help them and offer more than other sites. Some of the best e-commerce sites develop 'stickiness' or ways of getting users to stay at the site for longer by including additional content beyond that which is strictly necessary to sell the product or service.

Additional information can enhance the commercial aims of the Web site by setting the travel or leisure experience within a more enticing context. Successful sites like www.ebookers.com use additional content from other sources to build their travel portals. ebookers' core product consists of flights, hotels, car rental and so on, which are promoted most directly. Another tier of enhanced product including a bookstore and newsletters enhances the site and promotes the product in a less explicit way.

The ebookers.com site then has an additional element that it describes as 'inspirational content'. This is not directly related to ebookers.com core product but helps to sell the idea of travel and helps to suggest reasons for travelling. This content includes weather reports and information from travel guides. The overall result is a site that inspires confidence and encourages users to book online.

USEFUL SITES

The Internet is a limitless and almost free source of advice, case studies, practical examples and information. The following is a random selection of Web sites mentioned in the main text of this book and which I think might be useful to tourism and leisure practitioners.

One of the best things about the Internet is that it is international, so you can easily access information which might otherwise not be available in every country.

Because of the fast-moving and changing nature of the Internet, none of these sites can be guaranteed to be as they were at the time of writing. Links get broken, sites disappear, are bought or not updated so this list should be taken as a starting point only. Inclusion of a Web site in the following listing does not constitute a formal recommendation.

GENERAL INFORMATION

www.howstuffworks.com

Lots of easy-to-understand technical explanations including ones about how the Internet and search engines work.

www.searchenginewatch.com

Extensive information about how search engines work and how to improve your rank in their listings. It also includes information such as listings of the different types of search engines and directories, with explanations of how each one operates.

www.linkpopularity.com

An easy way to find out which sites are linking to yours.

www.clickz.com

Information about marketing and advertising on the Internet.

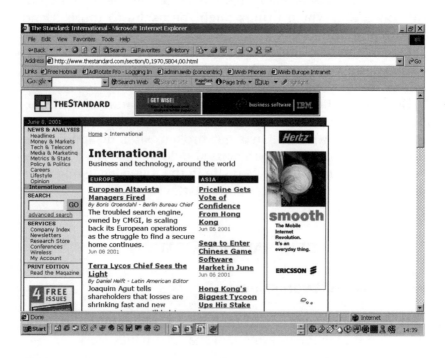

Figure 12.1   A huge amount of 'how to' and industry information is available free on the Internet

www.webpagesthatsuck.com

Amusingly titled useful site based on the premise that the best way to teach design is to show what doesn't work.

www.asa.org.uk

Advertising Standards Authority, with information on online and offline advertising.

www.Royalmail.co.uk

Includes useful advice on undertaking direct mail campaigns.

www.Marketingfile.com

Useful starting point to find mailing houses and list brokers since most of the largest companies are gathered together on this site.

www.Netbenefit.co.uk

Domain name registration company, and a good place to check which domain names are still available.

www.icann.com

Domain name registration body.

PR-RELATED RESOURCES

www.newsbureau.com
www.prWeb.com
www.pressreleasenetwork.com

www.Internetwire.com
www.ereleases.com

RESEARCH ABOUT INTERNET USERS

www.nua.ie
www.forrester.com
www.continentalresearch.com
www.jup.com
www.datamonitor.com
www.nopres.co.uk
www.caci.co.uk
www.thestandard.com/europe
www.digitrends.net
www.HenleyCentre.com
www.nielsennetratings.com

Figure 12.2 Sites like Forrester provide continually updated research information

MAPS

www.multimap.com

Enables users to search for place names, postcodes and travel directions.

www.streetmap.co.uk

Map site which allows users to zoom in on any UK area by entering a postcode, Ordnance Survey grid reference or telephone code.

www.ordsvy.gov.uk

Ordinance Survey site with information on maps, guides and digital map data.

www.rac.co.uk/services

The RAC's route planner and traffic news.

www.theaa.co.uk

Site for the Automobile Association.

TOURISM AND LEISURE-SPECIFIC ADVICE AND INFORMATION

www.tourismtrade.org.uk

Offers access to tourism intelligence with statistics for inbound tourism, demographic statistics about visitors to Britain, market profiles and information about the activities of the British Tourist Authority.

www.englishtourism.org.uk

The English Tourism Council's Web site which also links to www.staruk.org.uk, offering a wide variety of research material.

www.etp.org.uk

Site developed by the British Hospitality Association called Excellence Through People, giving employers examples of good practice and a directory of the best industry employers.

13

FREQUENTLY ASKED QUESTIONS

This chapter summarizes some of the most frequently asked questions about Internet marketing.

Q. There has been a lot of publicity recently about the demise of 'dot.coms'. Does that mean that the Internet is not as good as we thought it was?

A. The 'dot.coms' to which so much publicity refers are the myriad of new companies that have sprung up, hoping to make their fortune on the Internet. The majority of these seek to sell goods, ranging from clothes to books and holidays.

Many of these dot.coms are backed by venture capital and investment companies, in the hope that one day their shares will be publicly traded on the stock exchange and make vast returns for their backers. Unfortunately, many of these companies were overly optimistic and projected much faster returns and higher profits than have been possible. Many of them sought to sell goods that have not yet gained widespread acceptance on the Internet, such as clothes, which most people want to try on and feel before they buy. Many of the so-called dot.coms were set up without adequate market research and/or with limited business experience. Needless to say, these are the ones that have failed or are failing.

The one e-commerce sector that has exceeded all expectations has been travel. As chapter 3 indicates, tourism and leisure are ideal products and services for e-commerce.

It is important to make a distinction between using the Internet as one of several distribution channels and founding a business that relies solely on the Internet. Most of the failing dot.coms have done the latter.

Consumers like to be given a choice of ways of buying a product or service, and the Internet increases this choice. However, the fact remains that many people still want to buy face-to-face or to speak to a human voice. Companies with both an online and an offline presence seem to be more successful.

The Internet has another important function, which is the main subject of this book. It is an extremely powerful and cost-effective promotional method. Despite the negative publicity surrounding dot.coms, Internet usage is increasing dramatically among all sectors of society. Tourism and leisure companies that fail to use the power of the Internet as part of an integrated marketing strategy are missing out on a great new opportunity to reach an ever-wider marketplace.

Q. I've heard the comment 'the banner ad is dead' quite a lot lately. Is it true?

A. When banner ads first appeared on the Internet, average click-through rates reached as high as 30 or 40 per cent. This was clearly due to the novelty factor and relative scarcity of this type of advertising. With time, however, the novelty factor wore off and click-through rates settled to a figure of 1 or 2 per cent.

By virtue of the vast size of the Internet, there is now an abundance of places/sites (called 'inventory') on which to advertise. This increased supply has had the effect of pushing down CPM (cost per thousand impression) rates. This is good for the advertiser and not so good for Web site publishers.

Advertising on the Web is becoming increasingly concentrated in the hands of a very small group of sites. Recent research shows that 95 per cent of all advertising revenues are earned by only 50 sites worldwide. Many of these sites are search engines and directories.

Overall, online advertising is still growing faster than any other advertising medium and has already overtaken outdoor billboard advertising in its popularity.

Another factor to consider is that until now most online advertising has focused on the small banner format. Small banners offer a restricted size and format and do not always take advantage of the opportunity for interactivity, which is one of the strengths of the Internet. This is one of the reasons why new advertising formats are now being introduced.

Other lessons are being learnt, such as the need to change creatives more frequently, to make advertisements as interactive as possible and to engage customers more actively in the message of the advertisement. Banner ads are not dead, but evolving.

Q. I need to promote to people who do not use computers. It must surely be a waste of time trying to use the Internet to reach them?

A. The profile of people who are online is changing. Several years ago, young 'geeks' were far more likely to access the Internet than your granny. Now, one of the fastest-growing segments of Internet users is the 'silver surfer' group, who are more likely to include your grandmother. People who have never shown any interest in owning a computer are suddenly buying one for their home, and PC ownership is at an all-time high.

Add to this the fact that the Internet is increasingly available through other channels and devices such as mobile telephones and the television, and it will become obvious that Internet usage is still growing. It is possible to reach people via the Internet even when they never use a computer. Not everyone will be online and it will remain impossible to reach a minority of people via the Internet. But, as chapters 2 and 5 indicate, the Internet is becoming part of our lives.

However, you should be wary of using *only* the Internet to reach your customers; it is just one channel of distribution and one promotional tool among many others. For greatest effect, you should integrate use of the Internet in your overall marketing strategy and continue to use other promotional tools as well.

Q. People say that they keep trying to use the Internet but cannot find the information they are looking for. Will this always be the case?

A. Internet usage has grown at an incredible rate and the amount of information available online has expanded exponentially. The major search engines and directories have been largely incapable of keeping up with the number of new sites so only around 30 per cent of all Web sites are catalogued by them.

This does mean that unless you know the domain name of specific sites, it can be difficult to find information. Until now, the search engines and directories have not been particularly intuitive to use. 'Bots' are now gaining importance and several companies are working to develop and improve them to make the Internet easier to navigate. These are intelligent agents that incorporate rule-based artificial intelligence systems, so they can recognize key phrases and respond to particular enquiries. This means that instead of scrolling down a long block of information, Internet users can interrogate certain sites to find the information they are looking for.

The Web site www.askjeeves.com uses this type of technology to offer a type of search engine that many users find much more intuitive. Call centres will also be able to take advantage of a voice-based version of this technology to respond to the most frequently asked questions.

When you develop or improve your site, be aware that many people find it difficult to access the information they are looking for. Many of us are now suffering from information overload to some extent, so it is important to layer and prioritize information and not to try to provide everything at once in one block. A useful way of doing this is to think carefully about the different types of people likely to use your site and the different reasons for doing so, and to offer a variety of ways of accessing the same information.

Q. Some of my customers say they will not use the Internet because they prefer the personal touch. What do you think?

A. There are undoubtedly still some barriers to overcome before everyone feels comfortable using the Internet. Even when these have been overcome, some people will only use the Internet for certain tasks and prefer to undertake others on the phone or face-to-face.

Two things are likely to happen. One is that more and more people will research information on the Internet and then go elsewhere to actually buy or make a booking. For example, the Internet offers an amazing range of destination-specific information that is almost impossible to find elsewhere so quickly and cheaply. However, it can be difficult to actually book holidays online and many people want the reassurance of human interaction, so they will still prefer to go to a travel agent or other intermediary, having used the Internet for preliminary research.

The other thing that is already happening is that Webmasters are taking account of the need for human contact and providing it within their Web sites. 'PhoneMe' is one of several companies that offers a free call-back facility and a human response to customer requests. You may have seen a 'PhoneMe' button on some Web sites, especially those selling more complicated products like mortgages. Consumers surf for initial information and then, when they have questions, they can click on this button. They are asked to enter their telephone number and when they would like to be called, including immediately. If they take the latter option, a few seconds later the phone will ring. A human voice answers any questions or concerns, guiding the consumer to a sale.

There are two ways you can help your customers feel more comfortable using your Web site if they are likely to miss a more personalized approach.

The first of these is to ensure that you always provide all your contact details in a prominent place within your site and that you provide plenty of information about the company and people behind the Web site. This could include photographs (try to make them more interesting ones than passport-style 'mug shots') of all the staff and include brief descriptions that make them sound more human.

The second relates to the style in which you write the content for your Web site. Avoid writing too formally and try to write in the same style as you would speak directly to your customers, injecting humour and a warm style whenever possible.

Q. How can I make my customers trust my site when they are worried about issues like privacy and security?

A. Some customers will never be comfortable about buying or making bookings online, and you need to accept this and provide them with other options such as telephone booking. However, many more will be more likely to trust your site if you take these simple steps to reassure them:

■ Ensure that information about your company is prominently displayed and makes your services feel as tangible as possible. The earlier suggestion about including staff photographs is part of this approach.

■ Offer several ways of booking and alternative payment systems, such as the option to print off and fax a form including credit card numbers or to make a telephone booking.

■ Explain exactly how your system works, outlining any arrangements you have made to protect the customers' security and what sort of redress they have if anything goes wrong. If you can offer some sort of guarantee, do so.

■ Reassure your customers by including a privacy statement and other relevant information on your site. There are examples of these in chapter 11.

GLOSSARY

Active Server Page (ASP) A Web page created using various scripts (mini-programs for Web sites) and programming languages.

Ad server Software that delivers advertisements to relevant Web site pages and keeps track of advertising inventory and performance.

Ad views/impressions Number of times a page with an online advertisement on it has been viewed.

Application Service Provider (ASP) A Web site that manages and distributes software-based services and solutions to customers.

Attachments Multimedia files that are 'attached' to an e-mail. They may contain text, graphics, sound, video, spreadsheets or a database.

Avatar A graphical icon that represents a real person in a cyberspace system.

Backbone A major central high-speed network established by a company or organization for connecting smaller networks.

Back-end system   Any part of a Web site with which the user has no direct contact, such as automated credit card processing or distribution system.

Bandwidth   The capacity for traffic on any computer network (including the Internet) or the maximum amount of information passed over a connection in one second, usually measured in bps (bits per second).

Banner ads   The most popular advertising method, usually a rectangular shape across the top of the host Web site, with a link to more information or another Web site.

Bookmark   Virtual bookmarks work in the same way as real ones. They record a Web site or URL so you can go straight to it at a later date.

Browser   Viewer for the World Wide Web or, in other words, window through which the Internet is viewed. The most popular are Microsoft's Internet Explorer and Netscape's Navigator.

Caching   This is the process of storing frequently requested information either on a server or on special sites within a network to avoid 'traffic jams' on the web at peak access times.

Chatroom   An online facility for real-time communication between people over the Internet, usually achieved through typed conversations.

Cheque Guarantee Service

An application that establishes financial information about a customer before allowing (or disallowing) a transaction.

Click

Click (or double click) of the computer mouse to access information via a link.

Clicks-and-mortar

Name for companies that have both offline (for example, High Street) and online trading operations.

Click-through rates

The click-through rate measures the number of times an advertisement is clicked on, so is effectively a way of measuring interest in an advertisement.

Common Gateway Interface (CGI)

A way of transferring information between a Web server and a CGI program. A CGI program is any program designed to accept and return data.

Cookie

A cookie is a piece of software that records information about users. It holds this information until such time as the server requests it. For example, if you are browsing around a virtual shop, each time you place an item in your basket the information is stored by the cookie until you decide to buy and the server requests the purchase information.

CPM

The cost per thousand advertisement impressions is the usual measure for online advertising.

Domain name

The Web site address or Universal Resource Locator, part of the naming hierarchy of the Internet.

Domain server (DNS)

A server that performs address verification on the Internet, finding the right computer to connect to for access to Web sites and e-mail.

Extranet

A Web-style network that is used by a specific, but often broad range of people such as a group of suppliers and customers, or a particular industry. It often branches off a company's internal network.

File extension

Commonly a three- or four-letter extension to the end of a file name designating the file type. There are hundreds in existence and new ones are constantly being invented. Examples are: .txt (text file), .gif (Graphics Interchange Format).

File Transfer Protocol (FTP)

A method used to transfer computer files from one computer to another over the Internet. It usually refers to the process of transferring HTML files and graphics files (such as GIF and JPEG) from your computer to the computer that hosts your Web site.

Firewall

A means of protecting Web sites and systems from trespassers and 'hackers'. A firewall is a secure software barrier against unauthorized intrusion or data theft.

Flash

A technology developed by Macromedia to create small (in terms of file size) animations.

Frequently Asked Questions (FAQs)

Lists of frequently asked questions (and their answers) allow the user to search for a query that somebody has already found the answer to. Many Web sites now have an FAQ section, cutting down on some of the need for customer-service call centres.

Graphics Interchange Format (GIF)

Developed by Compuserve, GIF is a platform-independent file format, used extensively throughout the Internet for graphics files. It compresses files using a 'lossless' method that ensures picture quality is not diminished.

Hit

Entry in the log file of a Web server, generated each time a request is made. This is not the same as users, visitors or pages.

Home page

The first page a surfer sees when they run their browser.

Host

You usually connect to a host computer whenever you use the Internet.

Hyperlink

Hyperlinks are highlighted text or images that, when selected (usually by clicking the mouse button), follow a link to another page. Hyperlinks can also be used to automatically download other files as well as sound and video clips.

Hyper Text Mark-up Language (HTML)

The language of the web, HTML is the code inserted in a file intended for display on a Web browser to indicate how and what should be displayed.

Hypertext Transport Protocol (HTTP)
Used on the World Wide Web since 1990, this application-level protocol is essential for the distribution of information throughout the Web.

Image map
An image with clickable 'hot spots', allowing several hyperlinks from a single image file. For example, the image could be of a country, split into different areas, each of which could be clickable and will hyperlink to a larger view of that specific area, or link to further information about each area.

Integrated Services Digital Network (ISDN)
Digital telephone lines enabling faster data transfer rates than using analogue lines. They allow simultaneous transfer of voice, data and video information.

Internet Service Provider (ISP)
A company that supplies access to the Internet.

Interstitials
Advertisements that pop up between Web pages. So far they have not proved very popular because they can irritate users and slow page loading times.

Intranet
A Web-style network that sits within the boundaries of a single company. However, many intranets span more than one location (for companies with more than one office) and/or can be accessed from anywhere.

IP address
This number refers to the physical location of individual Web or mail servers. Domain names provide

aliases for these which are much easier to understand, for example www.Websitename.com rather than 104.66.27.33. While many domain names can apply to one computer, a computer can have only one IP address.

Java

An application language developed by Sun Microsystems to work on any platform (Windows, Mac, UNIX, etc) that allows applications on different platforms to talk to one another. Java is a Web programming language supporting online multimedia effects, such as simple cartoon-like animation, background music and continuously updated information in Web pages.

Javascript

A simple version of Java, developed by Netscape for Web page controls (such as buttons that highlight when you roll the cursor over them).

Joint Photographic Experts Group (JPEG or .jpeg)

A standard of image compression developed especially for use on the Internet. Most photographic images can be highly compressed using this method, without greatly diminishing image quality.

Leased line

A telephone line that is rented and therefore dedicated to the user, unlike 'normal' lines that are paid for through call charges and therefore effectively shared. These are usually given over to a specific task such as Internet data transfer, as they are permanently connected between two points.

Links
Links are the connections between hypertext pages. Every time you click on highlighted text to go to another page you are following a link.

Local Area Network (LAN)
A computer network that occupies a small area. Most LANs are confined to a single building or group of buildings. However, one LAN can be connected to other LANs over any distance via telephone lines and radio waves.

Menu
Used for navigating Web pages, the menu is usually a list of options and links appearing on the home page of a Web site.

Meta tags
HTML tags that surround certain words so that search engines can identify keywords when performing a search.

Microsite
A small site or sub-site usually contained within a larger Web site, often designed for a specific purpose such as responding to particular enquiries.

Modem
A device used to connect most home users to the Internet, a modem is the interface between the user's computer and telephone line. It is short for modulator/demodulator.

Motion Picture Experts (MPEG)
Video compression format used for movie or animation clips on the Internet.

Netiquette
Informal, largely undocumented set of rules designed to make the Internet a polite and civilized 'society'.

Network

Any number of computers that have been interconnected to allow information to be transferred among them, ranging from a small office to the Internet itself.

Newsgroups

Similar to a mailing list. Subscribers to a newsgroup can contribute to the list and are often encouraged to do so. Newsgroups usually (but not always) have a moderator, who is there to keep order and can bar people if they become abusive.

Opt-in mailing

A mailing sent to pre-qualified groups of people, who have agreed to be on a mailing list.

Pixel

Short for 'picture element', a pixel is a single point or 'dot' in a graphics image. The number of pixels decides the picture density or quality. The more pixels, the clearer the image.

Plug-ins

Plug-ins are programs that can be installed and used as part of your Web browser. Although they are generally easy to download, many surfers resist using them. Shockwave and RealAudio are examples of plug-ins required for audio and video.

Portal

A term for Web sites that have all the services people are likely to use online such as search engines, chatrooms and online shopping. They are all gathered together on one site.

Post Office Protocol (POP)

Provides a store-and-forward service, intended to move e-mail on demand from an intermediate server to a single destination machine, usually a PC or Macintosh.

Protocol Standards governing the transfer of information between computers.

Rich Media A means of including multimedia such as sound and possibly video. Rich Media is increasingly popular with advertisers.

Search engines Term often used to describe sites like www.yahoo.com or www.lycos.com that help users search the Internet for information.

Server Computer or software on a computer that allows other computers to access it via a network or over the Internet.

Short Message Service (SMS) The transmission of short text messages to and from a mobile phone.

Signature file The automatic addition of a few lines at the foot of an e-mail. These usually consist of the sender's e-mail address, full name and other details.

Spam Unwanted or 'junk' e-mail.

Spider Spiders are sent out by various search engines to search the Web for information on Web sites.

Streaming Video or audio files sent in compressed form over the Internet and displayed on the viewer's screen as it arrives.

Tag

In HTML terms, a 'tag' is used for marking-up text or coding it in various ways so that it is formatted in a Web document. They are sometimes called 'markup tags'.

Unique users

Number of individuals who visit a site within a specified period of time. It is more useful to keep a record of how many users a site has than how many 'hits' it gets, since some bad sites have a high number of hits because of bad navigation.

Universal Resource Locator (URL)

The Web site address or domain name.

Upload

Transfer of files from a local computer to a specified remote computer (as opposed to download where files are pulled off a remote machine). Once a Web site has been developed, it has to be uploaded to a host so the site can be seen by all Internet users.

Virus

A virus is similar to a 'bug' caught by humans, and can attack computers and hide anywhere a computer stores information. Viruses have the ability to transfer from computer to computer via e-mail or the Internet and various other networks. A virus can do a number of things to a recipient such as reformatting hard drives or destroying data.

Visit

A user's interaction with a site within a specified time period, which considers all the pages seen on the same site during one session in a given period of time. It is the sequence of hits that constitute a visit at a predetermined period of time, usually timed out after 30 minutes.

Vortal
A vertical portal or an industry specific or specialist Web site.

Webmaster
The person responsible for maintaining a Web site.

Wide Area Network (WAN)
Any network that exists in more than one physical location. Typically, a WAN consists of two or more local area networks (LANs). The Internet is the biggest WAN of all.

Wireless Application Protocol (WAP)
Specification that allows users to access information via any handheld wireless device such WAP-enabled mobile phones.

INDEX